NEWCASTLE/BLOODAXE POETRY SERIES: 8

RUTH PADEL:

SILENT LETTERS OF THE ALPHABET

NEWCASTLE/BLOODAXE POETRY SERIES

NEWCASTLE/BLOODAXE POETRY LECTURES

In this innovative series of public lectures at Newcastle University, leading contemporary poets speak about the craft and practice of poetry to audiences drawn from both the city and the university. The lectures are then published in book form by Bloodaxe, giving readers everywhere the opportunity to learn what the poets themselves think about their own subject.

NEWCASTLE/BLOODAXE POETRY SERIES: 8

RUTH PADEL

Silent Letters
of the Alphabet

NEWCASTLE / BLOODAXE POETRY LECTURES

BLOODAXE BOOKS

ISBN: 978 1 85224 827 8

First published 2010 by
Newcastle Centre for the Literary Arts,
Newcastle University,
Newcastle upon Tyne NE1 7RU,
in association with
Bloodaxe Books Ltd,
Eastburn,
South Park,
Hexham,
Northumberland NE46 1BS.

Second impression 2014

www.bloodaxebooks.com
For further information about Bloodaxe titles
please visit our website or write to
the above address for a catalogue.

Supported by
**ARTS COUNCIL
ENGLAND**

Cover design: Neil Astley & Pamela Robertson-Pearce.

Printed in Great Britain by Bell & Bain Limited, Glasgow, Scotland, on
acid-free paper sourced from mills with FSC chain of custody certification.

Contents

Acknowledgements

Many thanks to the Departments of English and Creative Writing at Newcastle University, for inviting me to give these lectures in May 2008, in a week which demonstrated magnificently how poetry can draw together many different people from many different places in a city.

When the lectures became written up as a book, their title mutated and I have chased various themes much further as a result of valuable comments from the audiences, whom I also want to thank.

I am grateful to the Dún Laoghaire Poetry Now International Festival, too, for inviting me to give their Keynote Address in the same year. Some of the ideas developed there, and comments from that audience, also found their way into this book.

Very many thanks to Robert Douglas-Fairhurst, Elaine Feinstein and Angela Leighton for illuminating and generous comments, to Nicholas de Lange for inspirational advice on Hebrew, and to Colin Higgins, Librarian at Christ's College, Cambridge.

Thanks also to the Leverhulme Foundation and Christ's College Cambridge for an Artist in Residence Bursary which bought me time to write these lectures up, a room to do it in, and a delightful society of scholars and students who enriched the writing.

Finally I'd like to thank Linda Anderson who encouraged and supported the project, and Neil Astley, who has done so much for poetry in the British archipelago and beyond, for patient, erudite and sympathetic editing.

For George and Zara Steiner
much love

The Aleph is a silent letter and thus easy to pronounce.
DICTIONARY OF BIBLICAL HEBREW

On Metaphor and Saying Otherwise

Image and Silence

'I hate poets,' a newspaper editor once said to a friend of mine. 'They never say what they mean.' Maybe he disapproved of the idea that words in a poem mean *more* than they say. Maybe, from where he stood, it seemed a kind of trick. But part of the pleasure in reading a good poem is enjoying working out the unspoken things. There is no single correct reading; we all respond to different unsaid things. Often the differences between readers are widest, and the things unsaid are the most crucial, when we encounter images.

Louis MacNeice talks about imagery in his essay *Varieties of Parable* and uses 'parable' as an umbrella term for all types of image, simile, allegory, emblem, symbol and metaphor.[1] Parable, he says, is 'double level writing', a kind of 'sleight of hand'. Which also suggests tricks.

I too shall lump the different varieties of image under one master word. Mine is metaphor, not parable. But a glance at the names of some of the others explains why someone who distrusted poetry anyway might feel that of all things poetry does, the worst area of double dealing is the imagery.

'Allegory' comes from *alle*, 'other', and *agoreuein*, 'to speak in the market-place (*agora*)'. *Allegoria* came to mean 'allegorical inter-pretation' or 'veiled or metaphorical language', but essentially it is a way of speaking 'otherwise' than in public. Something different, more secret, than what gets said in the market-place.

'Parable' gets at a similar idea from a different angle. *Para* means 'aside' or 'beside', *paraballein* is 'to throw beside, set against or alongside', *paraballomai* is 'I deceive, betray'. The adjective *parabolos* describes a thing or act that goes astray, or turns aside from the straight safe path: 'dangerous, reckless, deceitful'. *Parabole*, literally 'a throwing beside', comes to mean 'comparison', 'analogy', 'obliquity'. And, in the New Testament, 'parable'.

The *agora* is a news editor's home patch. In its light, detour and silence look like deceit. Maybe he mistrusted the notion that going away from what you are talking about gets you closer to it, for that is what many good poems do. C.K. Williams' poem 'Tar', for instance, which focusses on workmen stripping a roof, is a profound political poem about a nuclear-reactor accident and the realisation ('however much we didn't want to, however little we would do about it, we'd understood') that one day the nuclear will get us all. 'We were going to perish of all this, if not now, then soon, if not soon, then someday.' But it ends with what the neighbourhood boys do with the tar left by the roof-workers. 'Every sidewalk on the block was scribbled with obscenities and hearts.'

Finally, the editor may have wanted to control all the meanings his readers find in his paper. But a good poem wants to free up meanings, suggest new ones which may indeed 'turn aside' from the public eye, and set going in its readers any number of unspoken resonances, just like those 'obscenities and hearts'. In the words of W.S. Graham, the power a good poem has is the power of 'release'. The 'purpose' of a poem, he says, 'is that it can be used by the reader to find out something about himself'.[2]

What I want to explore in these lectures lies at the heart of what that editor mistrusted in poetry: the unsaid. How do poems use silence? Why is writing them the art not only of putting words together, but also of not saying? How is it that reading poems well means responding to what they do not say as well as what they do?

Writing a poem, if you cut out an over-explicit word, you often find that it has more effect. It works better by not being there. The meaning of a poem is the poem, sum of all its sounds, words, relationships, images, movements and implications. You don't want a loudly explanatory word in there, tying things down. As Graham puts it, 'The meaning of a poem is itself, not less a comma.' What a good poem is 'about' is always a complicated question. It is often something the poem does not actually say. 'The poem is more than the poet's intention,' says Graham. 'The poet does not write what he knows but what he does not know.'[3]

If you could have said in advance what the poem means, you

would not have written it. Writing is discovering. A good poem says something beyond what you knew beforehand, and that 'beyond' is often reached by an image. For, as Wallace Stevens said, you can't 'get beyond the images'.

I'm going to assume that the image and the unsaid belong together. That one entails the other.

The Grass Divides

The poem by Emily Dickinson beginning 'A narrow Fellow in the grass,' was one of the few printed in her lifetime. *The Springfield Daily Republican* published it in 1866, apparently without her knowledge and under a clunking title, 'The Snake'. She later said the poem was stolen from her. She could never have wished that title on it: its form is a riddle whose answer word, 'snake', is a silent presence gliding through the words just as the creature glides unseen through the grass.

But what also glides through this poem unspoken, is a way of looking at the world which represents ways of responding to a poem.

A narrow Fellow in the grass
Occasionally rides –
You may have met him – did you not
His notice sudden is –

The Grass divides as with a Comb –
A spotted shaft is seen –
And then it closes at your feet
And opens further on –

[…]

Several of Nature's People
I know, and they know me –
I feel for them a transport
Of cordiality –

But never met this Fellow
Attended, or alone
Without a tighter breathing,
And Zero at the Bone –

The first stanza deals in encounters: between snake and human, poem and reader. 'Fellow' suggests approachable humanity: kinship, as in fellow creature. Maybe it also nods to Satan disguising himself as a snake in Eden. Used of people, 'narrow' suggests someone closed to new ideas (in New England, apparently, it can also mean stingy, close with money), and the musical closeness of 'narrow' and 'Fellow' suggests being 'narrow' is essential to whatever this creature is.

The inverted word-order of the fourth line begins to close the gap between noticing snakes in the meadow and noticing things in a poem. Self-referentially, it draws attention to 'notice'. You 'notice' something in a poem, between the words perhaps, as you notice something in slots opened where 'Grass divides'. What you see there is 'spotted'; which highlights not only the snake's colouration but also (to spot is to notice) the noticing.[4] 'Shaft', strange word for a curvy snake, also suggests illumination, a 'shaft' of light. As you read a poem, spaces of insight open up, then again 'further on', through which you find the insights it will offer you.

This poem's two central stanzas, which I have not included, disclose 'a Whip lash'. There it is, 'Unbraiding in the Sun', then suddenly 'gone'. By the end, what you have seen is the record of a passage. Of, let's say, a meaning. You almost never see the thing itself, only an image for it (or of it). When you do, it changes you: your breathing is tighter.

One thing this poem seems to be about is how glimpsing, or insight, affects the observer. There is knowing ('nature's people') and being known ('they know me'). Places open in the poem but also in the reader. 'Zero at the bone' glances back to 'where grass divides'; the place for understanding which opens as you read is deep in yourself. The poem's unsaid word may stand for any unspoken meaning which has power to change your inner being.

The Magic of Distance

Metaphor is not poetry's monopoly. It is one of the big natural adventures of all language. Science and philosophy depend on it too. 'Our ordinary conceptual system,' says the linguist George Lakoff, 'in terms of which we both think and act, is fundamentally metaphorical in nature.' Jonathan Miller deals with language as theatre director as well as scientist. 'Finding out what something is,' he has said, 'is largely a matter of discovering what it is like. The most impressive contribution to the growth of intelligibility has been made by applying metaphors.'

William Golding pictures the beginning of this process in *The Inheritors*. His doomed Neanderthal discovers metaphor as a conceptual tool which helps him make sense of his changing world when invaded by *homo sapiens*.

> Lok discovered 'like'. He had used likeness all his life without being aware of it. Fungi on a tree were ears... In a convulsion of understanding Lok found himself using likeness as a tool as surely as ever he had used a stone to hack at sticks or meat. Likeness could grasp the white-faced hunters with a hand, could put them into the world where they were thinkable and not a random and unrelated irruption.[5]

George Eliot, however, reproaches Aristotle for his unalloyed enthusiasm for metaphor. Why didn't he temper his praise with a lament, 'that intelligence so rarely shows itself in speech without metaphor – that we can so seldom declare what a thing is, except by saying it is something else?'[6]

Where does this leave poets?

On a flight to Russia in 1983, the Irish poet Paul Durcan looked down at the Caucasus mountains.

'They look like tents,' he said to his colleague Anthony Cronin.

'Paul, would you ever stop saying things are *like* things?' said Cronin. 'They either are, or they're not.' Durcan has not used the word 'like' in a poem since.[7]

What are you doing when you connect mountains and tents by 'like'? You see mountains more freshly when you compare them to something else, but what happens if (moving from simile to metaphor) you take the 'like' away? If, as George Eliot points out we are doing, you say they actually *are* something else? How much does 'like' matter? Keeping it, you stay on some fence between a momentary shift of perspective and a permanent transformation. But to poets at least, dropping it can feel violent and daring. You are committed to strangeness. You have jumped into the permanent, into the other world.

Some sense of another world is crucial to poems, and it is particularly metaphor which helps gets you there. Poems can work fine without metaphors, yet metaphor seems central to poetry. Why?

I think because metaphor and poetry have in common a kind of outward restlessness. Adrienne Rich suggests that poetry never rests on 'the given' but will always move on from 'the found place, the sanctuary'.[8] Metaphor does that too. Both poems and metaphors open new possibilities of seeing. In Keats, the nightingale's song opens for the listener 'magic casements on the foam / Of perilous seas'. Poems open windows, make you look out and see new, and metaphor is a potent way of doing that. Seeing new, making you see more sharply what something is by calling it something else, is metaphor's speciality. It is what Durcan was up to above the Caucasus.

Emily Dickinson pictures poetry as a house with more windows and better doors than prose.

I dwell in Possibility –
A fairer House than Prose –
More numerous of Windows –
Superior – for Doors – [9]

Maybe what metaphor does for a poem is let you look out from its structures (a 'stanza' is a 'room') while enjoying being in them. Like a modulation in music, a metaphor moves you away from the poem's home key. Like poetry itself, its possibilities disorientate; metaphor can make you suddenly and enjoyably a stranger in your linguistic world. We might take Dickinson's windows and doors as metaphors for metaphor, because metaphor is what you have to use if you want to reveal what metaphor does.

Most people, though, picture metaphor as a form of travel. Lorca called it 'the equestrian leap that unites two worlds'. Standard metaphors for metaphor evoke both a distance between two things and physical movement across them. Metaphor is energy and movement. Movement out and also movement between. The Greek word *metaphora* comes from *meta*, 'across', and *pherein*, 'to carry'. Its Latin equivalent is *translatio*, 'translation.' Both mean 'carrying across'.

The history of unpacking this metaphor for metaphor begins with Aristotle. In the *Poetics*, Aristotle defines *metaphora* by the related word *epiphora* (also from *pherein*), which by his day had the abstract meaning 'application' but which originally meant 'carrying towards'. Metaphor, he says, is the *epiphora* of a 'foreign' word (*allotrios*, 'alien', 'other') carried over to a 'home' place, *oikeion*, the word's 'normal', 'original' meaning.[10]

Alive inside this definition is the movement of sea trade, the chief source of ancient Greek prosperity. Metaphor's energy is the energy of relationship. Metaphor enriches by moving between home and foreign, self and other.

When I first went to Greece in 1970, I saw Aristotle's definition in action. I was a classics student but trying to learn modern Greek, in that state of learning a language when you are abnormally sensitive to images which native speakers take for granted. Everywhere on the streets I saw little three-wheeled vans which said METAPHORAI, 'metaphors', on their fronts. I asked the driver of one of them what his job was, what he did. 'I carry things,' he said, 'from one place to another.' Here was Aristotle's definition of metaphor, with the same mercantile undertones (wheels, though, rather than sails), loose on the Athenian streets.

Those vans are long gone (Greece has moved on) but they gave me my visual image of metaphor. I.A. Richards took Aristotle's image further by calling the two elements of metaphor a 'tenor' and a 'vehicle'. I just remember those vans and see three things in one: a common mode of transport, a box to be shifted and a new place to take it to.

Seamus Heaney's essay 'Mossbawm' describes how he hid as a boy in a hollow tree where he felt 'at the heart of a different life' and saw his 'familiar yard' differently, 'as if behind a pane of strangeness'. Heaney writes wonderfully about creativity and here he links it with a shift in the relationship between the security of the familiar and 'the challenges and entrancements of what is beyond'.[9] He is putting at the heart of creativity a procedure which belongs to metaphor, of seeing 'home' from a foreign perspective. Metaphor is not only a momentary conjuring trick which turns one thing into another in a single poem, but a more permanent form of magic, a principle of translation which lies at the core of creativity: seeing the world otherwise.

Heaney encapsulates this process in his poem 'Making Strange'.

I stood between them,
the one with his travelled intelligence
and tawny containment,
his speech like the twang of a bowstring,

and another, unshorn and bewildered
in the tubs of his wellingtons,
smiling at me for help,
faced with this stranger I'd brought him.

Then a cunning middle voice
came out of the field across the road
saying, 'Be adept and be dialect,
tell of this wind coming past the zinc hut,

call me sweetbriar after the rain
or snowberries cooled in the fog.
But love the cut of this travelled one
and call me also the cornfield of Boaz.

Go beyond what's reliable
in all that keeps pleading and pleading,
these eyes and puddles and stones,
and recollect how bold you were

when I visited you first
with departures you cannot go back on.'
A chaffinch flicked from an ash and next thing
I found myself driving the stranger

through my own country, adept
at dialect, reciting my pride
in all that I knew, that began to make strange
at that same recitation.[12]

The poem is located beside something which was once a foreign
thing built on home ground, an American airfield erected next to
the Heaneys' farm during the war. It relates a moment long after-
wards when (as Heaney has explained) the poet picked up, from
what had become the local airport, an American colleague, the
Jamaican-born Louis Simpson. Outside the pub they ran into a
Derry farmer, the poet's father as it happened. In the local dialect,
'making strange' meant to react defensively, so the title itself mod-
ulates between a local meaning (what the poet's father was doing)
and other wider meanings.

The poet is standing where poetry emerges, between the home
and the foreign. Like trans-lation – the 'carrying across' whose
Greek translation is *metaphora* – the voice of poetry is about between-
ness, about crossing boundaries (*middle voice, across the road*). You
hear the 'reliable' home territory 'pleading', but you have to make

departures, adventure into the foreign. This is about the mystery of being drawn to making a poem. The process involves magic ('adept', the alchemist's word, more mystical, less of a trick than MacNeice's sleight of hand) and distance. 'Dialect' is language that belongs to one place, but also means 'speaking across, speaking between', from *dia*, another Greek preposition for 'across'. Once magic and distance are in place, the poet can get to work.

This is metaphor at work as a creative principle, an outward urge. Writing a poem, you re-see 'all' you 'knew'. You see strange, make strange, and find yourself suddenly driving 'the stranger' through your 'own country'.

But you cannot go back on this alchemy, of translation, of crossing into new territory, or into a new way of seeing the old. Somewhere, metaphor involves a 'not'. There are several dimensions to the negatives around metaphor. The simplest way of defining metaphor is to distinguish it from simile and say it 'compares without saying like'. Aristotle says one way of making it is not to give a word one of its 'home' attributes.[13] My sister was once planting seeds in little window-pots with her three-year-old son and said 'It's like gardening, isn't it?' He looked up at her. 'Then it's *not* gardening,' he said. Metaphor, therefore, can draw attention to a negative – to what is not there. 'The unreality of the seen brings reality to the seeing,' as Octavio Paz's poem 'Blanco' says. Heidegger, in his essay on Hölderlin, says the image 'lets the invisible be seen'.[14]

Dealing in the not seen and not said, metaphor works through implication and hint. It asks the reader to bring their own baggage to the table and to see things that are not immediately apparent.

The Art of Hint

At the beginning of the 20th century, modernism changed some ways in which most poems of the previous hundred years had been saying things, and thereby changed a few ways of not saying too.

In 1916 Ezra Pound explained how he had come to write his famous couplet haiku 'In a Station of the Metro'.

> The apparition of these faces in the crowd;
> Petals on a wet, black bough.[15]

He said he had wanted to convert into language what he had felt and seen under the Place de la Concorde. What he saw was 'splotches of colour' and it took two years 'trying to record the precise instant when a thing outward and objective transformed itself, or darts into a thing inward and subjective' to find the verbal 'equation' of his vision.[16]

A traditional haiku has three lines, of five, seven and five syllables, so the first line should end after 'apparition'. There should be a central line running run on to 'crowd', and then a third: 'petals on a bough'.

Pound has two lines, one each for the two elements of metaphor. Home first, foreign after. The turn-point between the lines embodies metaphor's move between seen and unseen. The last line, extended by two syllables, which are also two adjectives, tips the weight onto the foreign, the image.

In *Varieties of Parable*, Louis MacNeice suggests that the two American poets who brought modernism to British poetry used images differently. Eliot 'was not a great exploiter of metaphor', being 'more concerned with the inside of man than his outside'. MacNeice quotes Eliot's 'Journey of the Magi':

> And an old white horse galloped away in the meadow.
> Then we came to a tavern with vine-leaves over the lintel,
> Six hands at an open door dicing for silver –

As metaphor or symbol, says MacNeice, the gamblers and horse have nothing to do with the Magi, and yet they are not just decoration. 'They are significant; but why, they cannot say, any more than their author can.' Eliot's relation to his images, MacNeice suggests, is a sort of 'magical compulsion' which works on a poet through remembered objects or events, though the poet cannot explain why they have a special charge.

The Waste Land's images, however, MacNeice describes as arrogant. 'They think they are there in their own right. Eliot has indulged them.'[17] This sounds an odd thing to say, about the poem which liberated everyone by accumulating disconnected images, and the poet who used a 19th-century painter's term 'objective correlative' to describe how a single image can communicate feeling and embody a large nexus of ideas.

'Artistic inevitability,' said Eliot in an essay of 1919, lies in 'complete adequacy of the external to the emotion.'[18] By 'external', he meant concrete. Poems work better when they use a concrete image to reveal emotion rather than describing it. This is the basis of today's motto in Creative Writing classes, 'Show, don't Tell.'

But that advice hails from further back than Eliot. In the first two decades of the 20th century, Pound and Eliot were influencing each other all the time both in their poetry and in their ideas about poetry. Pound's *poetry* did not reach its most extraordinary form until after he had absorbed *The Waste Land*, while Eliot's *ideas*, about poetry, were radically influenced by Pound, the Imagist. It was Pound, in 1912, who laid the ground for Eliot's objective correlative and today's poetic practice. Economise on vocabulary, he said. 'Use no superfluous word, no adjective which does not reveal.' Be precise. 'Consider the way of the scientist, rather than the way of an advertising agent.' Focus on the concrete:

> Go in fear of abstractions. Don't use such an expression as 'dim lands of *peace*'. It dulls the image. It mixes an abstraction with the concrete. It comes from the writer's not realising that the natural object is always the adequate symbol.

He later added that the image was 'a radiant node or cluster...from which, and through which, and into which, ideas are constantly rushing'.[19]

MacNeice is not running Eliot down, simply arguing that Pound and Eliot used images for different purposes. Eliot's interest, he says, stayed 'inside', with the thing for which he found an image. (The 'home', in Aristotle's language.) Pound was an Imagist, however, and in Imagism 'the image acquires special value, rather than the thing of which it is an image'.[20] Pound throws the focus entirely outside onto the new, onto the image. In 'Station of the Metro', he draws attention to the image by extending the last line with a description of it: 'black' and 'wet'.

In relation to metaphor, as to other aspects of their lives and work, we might see Eliot and Pound as Mr Nice and Mr Dangerous. Eliot became Mr Establishment: externally as poetry editor at Faber, internally in the flow of his iambic line. He used English poetry's iconic blank verse pentameter, the line of Shakespeare, Milton and Tennyson, brilliantly for everything: spiritual reflection, pub dialogue, fragmentariness itself. The ambiguities of his early life and first marriage were smoothed over in a social process very like the aural fluidity of his line. In his public life, as in his poems, wildness was earthed and made decent.

Pound, however, was modernism's rough trade. He wanted poetry to be 'harder and saner..."nearer the bone" ' and his life was upsettingly nearer bone too. Metrically, as well: he said he wanted to smash open the iambic.

Metrical variation had been plentiful in English poetry from the Elizabethans onwards and this was not the first time that pentameters had been broken up and broken down to express the fractures and discontinuities of a speaker's mind, or of its relationship with the wider social world. Blake, Whitman and Dickinson had opened up the forms of poetry long before. But Pound wanted to fracture Victorian and Edwardian securities. 'To break the pentameter, that was the first heave,' he wrote retrospectively in 1941.[21]

How new the ground which modernism opened really was, is a question of debate. 'Make it new' can mean 'renovate' as well as 'innovate.' But Pound's Imagism, at least, was uncompromising. He does not mess around with 'like' – the faces *are* petals. We have left the premise and are in an unknown zone. This, perhaps, is Pound's main legacy to 'mainstream' poets today.

For British poets, Eliot and Pound were the revolution which became the foundation, like the revolution of evolution which is the basis of modern biology. But evolution is now rejected on emotional grounds by over half the world's population, and modernism too is more divisive now in British poetry than it was thirty years ago. Many readers violently reject modernist poetry and some poets violently reject any poem that does not follow the modernist agenda directly.[22]

Poetry today in Britain is wonderfully various, and poets divide sharply in what they have taken from modernism. All responsible contemporary poets in Britain stand somewhere on the shoulders of Eliot and Pound. But it is a question of where exactly they keep their feet (as it were) on these sloping scapulae. Today's neo-modernists follow Pound from the *Cantos* on, through American poets like Charles Olson, the Black Mountain poets and John Ashbery, and in Britain through W.S. Graham, Basil Bunting, J.H. Prynne and some of Geoffrey Hill, to name just the best-known. In many different ways they seem driven to say everything; to get all 365 degrees of experiencing the world into a poem. As Seamus Heaney has said of Ashbery, 'His subject is the nature of contemporary reality shifting away from you.'[23]

Mainstream poets, however, in Britain and Ireland, seem to have taken other things from modernism, above all Pound's ideas of scientific precision, and that the concrete image is enough to convey the emotion. I think, though, there is a third thing too. Pound's picture of unspoken ideas 'constantly rushing through' an image vividly reminds us that unspokenness is essential to metaphor. It is the image that makes a poem able to say the unsaid. Or, put it the other way round, the image is what allows a poem to leave unsaid what it is really saying.

Modernism made these uses of silence and metaphor newly alive in British poetry. But they were boosted from the 1960s by new metaphors, and their accompanying silences, in poems from two societies where not saying was literally life-saving.

First from the Soviet bloc, when images in poems by Mandelstam, Tsvetaeva, Akhmatova, Miłosz, Zbigniew Herbert and others, invented to slip under the censor's radar, were translated into English.[24]

And then a society closer to home.[25] Responding to the Troubles in Northern Ireland, Seamus Heaney drew on local Ulster strategies of silence along with metaphors from other cultures, such as the Bog People. In *North* (1975), the poem 'Kinship' speaks of 'legions' who 'stare / from the ramparts' (as, it did not need to say, British soldiers were doing in Ulster) and addresses the Roman historian Tacitus, witness to other massacres and legions. As a writer, Tacitus himself suggests silence: his literary style rests on his violent compressions and his name, of course, means 'Silent'.

Another poem from North, 'Whatever You Say, Say Nothing', speaks of a 'land of password, handgrip, wink and nod and the famous / Northern reticence, the tight gag / of place and times'. From now on, new adept art was coming from saying nothing, along with images of alien cultures, from Northern Irish communities where deadly violence, unseen until completed, was taken for granted. This was not poetry under censorship, but poetry which had reached a pitch of tact that matched how lives were lived in a place where there was only one issue and it did not need to be mentioned. 'Whatever you say, say nothing.'[26]

What has 'tact' to do with 'tacit'? They are not etymologically related but you cannot display tact without knowing how to be silent. Tact (which we shall look at more tomorrow) originally referred to 'touch'. It is skill in silence, a delicate handling. Which was exactly what Paul Muldoon, from the same landscape as Heaney, brought to younger British poets in the 1980s.

The British poets did not grow up with the dire *need* for tact that Ulster poets knew. But when Thatcher was changing political and social Britain, they found something they really needed in Muldoon's mastery of silence and implication, as well as in his slippery rhymes, yoking lines full of equally slippery absences. ('Why Brownlee left, and where he went, / Is a mystery even now.') Simon Armitage, and Carol Ann Duffy in collections like *Selling Manhattan*, spearheaded the way that poets who came to prominence in the late 80s invented their own ways of manipulating the unsaid, and questioning what readers took for granted politically, socially, erotically. You could sum up this revolution as the 'art of hint', the final phrase in David Harsent's poem, 'Art':

> Before this, I liked a sketchiness in art,
> figures, say three or four, half-done in white on almost-white,
> or something much like a bruise
> seeping up through the wash, so you might make out,
> if you stood side-on to the thing, eye-hollows, a nose,
> or a mouth saying O–O–O: whites, but also blues
> deep enough to make mauve in moonlight or snowlight
> (was it?) and these few standing still, standing apart,
> but more at their backs, a hidden weight in the canvas.
>
> It's everywhere, now, in the city's broken stone, in the glint
> off smashed glass, in the much-told tale
> of the bombed-out house where someone peeled off the wall
> a face stuck flat that came away whole
> still wearing the puckish stare of the hierophant,
> just a touch or two left on the whitewash, the art of hint.[27]

This sonnet is swollen in the middle by a fifteenth line with no rhyming partner: 'but more at their backs, a hidden weight in the canvas'. This line is itself the 'weight' at the poem's centre. Its figures 'weigh' this 'canvas', this incomplete picture of a war-smashed city, but they are unseen. The only way to make 'art' in this terrible context is by 'hint'. The most repeated word is 'white' (echoed distortedly at the poem's centre by 'weight'). One of the most-repeated sounds is O ('hollows', 'nose', 'O–O–O', 'mauve', 'snow', 'broken stone', 'told', 'whole') and though this is a block poem with no spaces, there is a strong sense of a blank O at the centre, visual image for the emotional blankness by which one holds off horror.

The picture (the 'art') is brokenness after catastrophe. But the poem is unbroken and complete. As a work of art it is raising the after-Auschwitz moral question – can you, should you, make *art*, a finished thing, out of destruction?

The last phrase is the poem's answer. Only 'hint' will do.

White Space

Harsent's O at the centre may gesture back to one of the 20th century's most famous war poems, Yeats's 'The Second Coming', which begins with the falcon's 'widening gyre', and in which 'things fall apart; the centre cannot hold'. But any blank also reminds us of the page on which poems appear.

Blank verse is lines with regular metre and line-length but no end-rhyme – as if rhyme were the only thing that gave a poem colour. But a blank can also be something not told. In Act 2 of *Twelfth Night* Viola tells Orsino that her father had a daughter who loved a man. 'What's her history?' he asked. 'A blank,' she says. 'She never told her love.' Which is a way of telling the audience that she loves Orsino, a telling by not-telling.

For poems, the visual correlative of what is not said is white space on the page. Spaces at the end of lines, spaces between stanzas and words, and space on a page where the poem makes and takes its being.

We can see that blankness behind the 'interrupting water' and 'spaces of sand' through which Bishop's sandpiper runs in his 'straight' line.

> The beach hisses like fat. On his left, a sheet
> of interrupting water comes and goes
> and glazes over his dark and brittle feet.
> He runs, he runs straight through it, watching his toes.
>
> – Watching, rather, the spaces of sand between them,
> where (no detail too small) the Atlantic drains
> rapidly backwards and downwards.[28]

The space between these two stanzas mirrors the movement of thought between them: one of those characteristic back-stitch self-corrections of Bishop's, which takes the poem forward while coiling the thought back. 'Rather', the self-refining word, is prefaced by 'Watching' and a forward-looking dash.

The whites at the end of a line, between stanzas (and also between words, as between the bird's 'dark toes'), mark the moments of pause visually. But they are also the poem's moments of most energy. The energy of turn, the wave-edge of one stanza, the move forward to the next.

That particular between-stanza space also marks the backward tug of water where the wave starts to drain back into sea. The bird is 'watching' this water, and his 'toes', and 'spaces of sand between', but the poem lets the reader see the water as a bigger grander thing: 'the Atlantic'. The whites of a poem are also a bigger grander thing than just bits of page the poem does not happen to cover.

Ted Hughes spotlights this white space with another animal in his six-stanza poem 'The Thought-Fox'. The first two stanzas are end-stopped. The first connects the forest outside with the poet's mind and waiting blank page. ('Something else alive / Beside the clock's loneliness / And this blank page where my fingers move.') The third stanza is not end-stopped: in its last two lines end with 'a movement, that now / And again now, and now, and now' which is followed by the fourth stanza's direct mention of snow. 'Sets neat prints into the snow.' By the end of the sixth stanza the tracks are set in both snow and poem. 'The page is printed.' Black on white. Words on the page, paw-prints of a wild animal that was there and is gone.

On stage, the light that matters is light that casts a shadow. A sculptor, facing a block of stone, also looks for the places of deepest shadow where the deepest cuts must go. 'The blacks' define what you are going to find in the stone, what you will make of it. Unlike words (at first glimpse, anyway), stone is a costly medium. You have to map the blacks carefully in advance. Once you've made a cut you can't go back.

Taking a poem in your hands, the spaces are white, not black. But black or white, what defines a form visually are hollows, shadows, gaps and spaces. In poems these also stand for the silences which shape it musically. White space is silence made visual: unseen and unsaid belong together.

Words *say*. But the poem also discloses unspokenly, through the words' relationships and spaces between them, other things than are said aloud. As you see shallow hollows in a landscape when the sun gets lower, the reader's imagination enters most actively into what is not said. We read the spaces and silences too. All our responses, conscious and unconscious, make up our experience of the poem.

The way we read poems today, both with ear and with eye, is not new. As soon as poems were written down, space and silence worked together in shaping them. Today's conventions are not the only kind. Charles Olson spaced his line with white pauses for the breath. So did Elaine Feinstein in her early work. Elizabeth Bishop's poem 'O Breath', one of her few published poems about the erotic female body, has a tongue-tied, erotically charged space running down its centre. A central reservation in the speaker's voice, as it were. Marking the path of what is ephemeral, human breathing, the poem questions whether any 'centre' can hold and uses Bishop's asthma to suggest the constrictions pressurising her poet's breath. In 1955, the airway where a woman could speak a love poem to another woman was pretty narrow and each phrase seems snatched from silence. Breath is caught and held across white spaces.

Beneath that loved   and celebrated breast,
silent, bored really   blindly veined,
grieves, maybe   lives and lets
live, passes   bets,
something moving   but invisibly,
and with what clamor   why restrained
I cannot fathom   even a ripple.
(See the thin flying   of nine black hairs
four around one   five the other nipple,
flying almost intolerably   on your own breath.)
Equivocal, but what we have in common's   bound to be there,
whatever we must own   equivalents for,
something that maybe I   could bargain with
and make a separate peace   beneath
within   if never with.[29]

Further back, there were the medieval scribes. Pound's *Cantos* talk about medieval scribes leaving blank spaces in their poems 'for the things they didn't know', which is one way of thinking about blank spaces written into any lineated poem. (Though what we know, of course, doesn't tell us how we come to know it.)

But in some Hebrew manuscripts, medieval scribes separated each line of verse into three blocks with spaces between. Like building a wall with the ends of each brick on the lower line positioned under the centre of the upper brick, they moved the spaces of the second line forward so its words fell under the spaces of the first, while its spaces were under the first line's words, creating a checker-board effect of words and space.

Shaped verse, like George Herbert's 'Easter Wings' – with 'wealth and store' appearing on the fattest line, 'most poore' and 'most thinne' at the thinnest, and 'O let me rise' coming as the wingspan grows – shows us how form itself is image. How we lay a poem out is metaphor too, another way of saying-without-saying.

> Lord, Who createdst man in wealth and store,
> Though foolishly he lost the same,
> Decaying more and more,
> Till he became
> Most poore:
>
> With Thee
> O let me rise,
> As larks, harmoniously,
> And sing this day Thy victories:
> Then shall the fall further the flight in me.
>
> My tender age in sorrow did beginne;
> And still with sicknesses and shame
> Thou didst so punish sinne,
> That I became
> Most thinne.
>
> With Thee
> Let me combine,
> And feel this day Thy victorie;
> For, if I imp my wing on Thine,
> Affliction shall advance the flight in me.

Emily Dickinson, by creating gaps, then dropping dashes into them like marks put on the window to stop birds flying into the glass, spotlit relations between words, and between the inside of a poem and the white space outside it, in a new individual way.

The Soul selects her own Society –
Then – shuts the Door –
To her divine Majority –
Present no more –

Unmoved – she notes the Chariots – pausing –
At her low Gate –
Unmoved – an Emperor be kneeling
Upon her Mat –

I've known her – from an ample nation –
Choose One –
Then – close the Valves of her attention –
Like Stone – [30]

Despite appearing porous, this poem is all about keeping out alien meanings. 'Close the valves of attention', bar from the soul – and from the enclave of a tiny poem, brave in its meshed but unpunctuated connectedness – all the world's emperors: public meanings, grandeur and rhetoric. The white spaces, the musical pauses, are filled. There is no chink for the unbounded space which provides the ground for the poem, and is a visual metaphor for the outside world, to intrude.

In his collection *The Eyes* (a title which spotlights the visual), Don Paterson has a poem called 'Poem' shaped like a bubble, which uses the white space round a poem as metaphor for what is outside.

'Poem' says it wants its words to sail away into the blue and pop. But what it actually does is to bound them in the nutshell of white space.

> I want neither glory
> nor that, in the memory
> of men, my songs survive;
> but still…those subtle worlds,
> those weightless mother-of-pearl
> soap-bubbles of mine…I just love
> the way they set off, all tarted up
> in sunburst and scarlet, hover
> low in the blue sky, quiver
> then suddenly pop[31]

The unmentioned white (not 'blue') defines the poem like surface tension, like skin.

But suppose 'Poem' is not words venturing out to space? Suppose it is white space, the pressure of silence, squeezing words into form? Is the bubble the words, or the space?

To those who yearn for the freeing-up of modernism, such a poem and such a question may feel obscene. Some forms of late modernism yearn to do away with containment. Marianne Moore's poem 'Poetry' calls poems 'imaginary gardens with real toads in them', but late modernism rejects any idea of garden, even a wild one. It wants poetry to bleed out into the world, into space.

Emily Dickinson and Don Paterson, however, in their different ways, suggest that one thing all poems may be "about" is the poem's relation to space around it and the world outside. Which is also the relation of words to the page, of said to unsaid and seen to unseen.

Where the Voice Belongs: the Beckett at the Gate

In *Going Home to Russia*, the collection Paul Durcan wrote after that Caucasus moment, 'home' is a lot of different things. It is Durcan's home, Ireland, which throughout this volume is constantly offering glimpses of the foreign, as in the poem 'A Vision of Africa on the Coast of Kerry'. It is also the foreign country, Russia, where the self-estranged poet finds poetry things, like Pasternak's grave, to identify with. Home and foreign are inside out. 'Foreign' offers you what the poet seems most at home with – poets, poetry, poems. Home is where he is most aware of the universe as alien, as foreign.

Another poem in that collection, 'The Beckett at the Gate', reminds us which previous Irish writer had made precisely this territory his own.

> That spring in Dublin
> You could not go anywhere
> Without people barking at you...
> 'Have you not been to the Beckett at the Gate?' [32]

By repeating the title phrase (in Beckettian manner) while shifting the capitals around, Durcan makes us re-see it.

> There's a beckett at the gate, there's a beckett at the gate...
> There's a Beckett at the gate, there's a Beckett at the gate...
> There's a beckett at the Gate, there's a beckett at the Gate...
> There's a Beckett at the Gate, there's a Beckett at the Gate...

What is this beckett at this gate? What is it about Beckett that matters so much to this poem and maybe to poetry?

One thing vital to Beckett is silence. On the one hand, there are the multiple silences, especially in the plays, which are also musical rests. Beckett came from a professional musical family. He was agonised when the first actors rehearsing *Happy Days* did not pause for as long as *he* heard the rests. But silence is also that emptiness in which his words are heard. One of Beckett's French poems starts and ends with the command to imagine – as if imagining is all we can put, or maybe all we can be, in this blank of a universe.

> imagine si ceci
> un jour ceci
> un beau jour
> imagine
> si un jour
> un beau jour ceci
> cessait
> imagine

Kevin Perryman translates this as:

> just think if all this
> one day all this
> one fine day
> just think
> if one day
> one fine day
> all this stopped
> just think [33]

Beckett wrote *Watt*, in English, in France during the war. Waiting, he said, for the war to end. After the war he went back to Ireland and realised he had to take a vow of lexical poverty.

> I realised that Joyce had gone as far as one could in the direction
> of knowing more, in control of one's material. He was always
> adding to it; you only have to look at his proofs to see that. I
> realised that my own way was in impoverishment, in lack of
> knowledge and in taking away, in subtracting rather than adding. [34]

In *Texts for Nothing*, he says we must

speak of things that don't exist, or only exist elsewhere, if you like, if you must, if you can call it existing. Unfortunately it is not a matter of elsewhere but of here.[35]

The great existential grief, the 'not a matter of elsewhere but of here', is that we cannot live permanently in the metaphor. We are not really at home in the foreign. If we were, we would lose the value of metaphor, there would be no more more mileage in relating the two things.

In 'Making Strange', Heaney pictures reliable home territory 'pleading and pleading', but although poetry involves departures into the foreign which you cannot go back on, Heaney's story of creativity comes from standing between Derry farmer and American visitor, then driving the 'stranger' through his 'own country' rather than making his home in the foreign. Eliot too, as MacNeice says, is interested more 'in the inside', the home thing imaged, rather than the foreign.

But just as imagery, in MacNeice's argument, is different for different writers, so where creativity emerges is different too. Maybe creativity comes from the way each of us is alert to metaphor and to relations between home and foreign.

Being civilised, being nice as well as dangerous, means you have to return, have to pay attention to the mountains as well as the tents. But for Beckett, after living the war in France, everything about foreign, both country and language, involved return and departure both at once. After Ireland, he went back to Paris and between 1946 and 1950 wrote his novel trilogy in the language-country where he could best fulfil his vow of impoverishment: French.

Maybe Durcan's 'beckett at the gate', some strange beast moving slow thighs outside Dublin in the spring, is the awareness that metaphor is all we have to go forward with. As Beckett says in *Texts for Nothing*, we have to 'get out of here and go elsewhere':

go where time passes and atoms assemble an instant, go where the voice belongs perhaps, where it sometimes says it must have belonged, to be able to speak of such figments.[36]

Maybe what the beckett says (baying, I imagine, at the gate) is that metaphor is the human condition. Or that our only way of dealing with who we are, in the world we have, is metaphor.

What helps is form. We are fox paws on snow, words on a page.

On Tone: or, What It Sounds Like
May Not Be What It Is

Tension

Yesterday we talked of silence as a musical tool, silence which shapes
the lines of a poem as shadow on a stage defines the characters.
And of another sort of silence, an emotional not-saying which you
could call a silence which represents the inward but at the same
time conceals it. As in Tennyson's lines from *In Memoriam*:

> Words, like Nature, half reveal
> And half conceal the soul within.

This silence of implication, something thought but not said, may
be political. Or simply politic, a silence due to tact or taste. It is
often playful too. The poem is keeping something to itself because
it wants the reader to have fun supplying it.

But the different sorts of silences belong together. Hegel argued
that human beings learned to speak when they learned how to
pause: that meaning came about from punctuation. 'What shall
Cordelia speak? Love, and be silent,' says Cordelia in *King Lear*.
Her pause at the question-mark is a musical necessity, but also en-
acts the politic silence we immediately hear about, of love not told.

A poem's social, emotional and political being is part of its status
as music. The politics (in the largest sense) and the sound are two
aspects of the same thing – tone.

Tone is a musical image. It reminds us that everything about
poetry's sense is also part of the way it sounds. Yesterday, in David
Harsent's poem about making art out of devastation, the other art
used to suggest how poetry might confront destruction was painting.

Today, exploring tone, what we need is music.

The Greek word *tonos*, 'a sound', from the verb *teinein*, to stretch, originally meant 'a stretching'. You get the pitch right by stretching a string on your kithara. Tuning it depends on tension. When the peg slips, the string slackens and your phorminx goes off key.

The most basic definition of tone in music is first of all a sound which you identify by its regular vibration and constant pitch: a sound you can put into harmonic relation with other similar sounds. Then, secondly, the quality of a sound. Every individual instrument and note has its own tone.

Moving on from music, tone is a healthy tenseness in any stretchable thing, a harp string, a body, muscles; any object which should have resilience and elasticity. Bodies, like rubber, can "lose" their tone.

In painting, tone is a quality of colour, the tint and shade. You can have many different tones of green, for instance, in one painting. Tone is also the effect produced by combining colour with light and shade.

More complicatedly, in human communication, tone is an intonation or modulation of voice which expresses a meaning or feeling; a tone of anxiety or contempt. Or a manner of speaking or writing which expresses a particular attitude. A friendly, say, or a cagey tone.

Tone is also the style and character of a place or of a society. The cheery tone of their kitchen, the prim tone of the late Victorian era.

People also use "tone" rather archly to mean a classy elegance. That brooch adds tone to your dress.

Four points running through these sorts of tone tell us a lot about tone in a poem.

1) Tautness, as of muscles.
2) Exactness of colour and pitch.
3) An outward thing, a sound or appearance, expressing something inward.
4) A balancing or combining of different elements.

Tautness, Number 1, seems to me to underlie all the others, at least it does in poems. Through 1 you reach 2 to 4: exact colour and pitch of words, the outward thing that perfectly suggests the inward, and different elements in play together.

Often, judging a poetry competition, I admire a poem I'm reading but then meet a word (usually an adverb or adjective) which lets the tone down and think Damn, I really wanted that poem to work. If the tone is not right, the poem will not work. Like violin pegs, it easily slips. Any slack word loses the tension. To keep the tension you have to cut the word. Silencing, it seems, makes a poem more taut.

Silent Pianos

'The Silent Piano', a poem by Louis Simpson whom we met yesterday as the unnamed foreigner in Heaney's poem 'Making Strange', shows 'inner life' expressed by unheard music when everything outside is, as in Harsent's poem, unspeakable.

> We have lived like civilised people,
> O ruins, traditions!
>
> And we have seen the barbarians,
> breakers of sculpture and glass.
>
> And now we talk of 'the inner life',
> And I ask myself, where is it?
>
> Not here, in these streets and houses,
> so I think it must be found
>
> in indolence, pure indolence,
> an ocean of darkness,
>
> in silence, an arm of the moon,
> a hand that enters slowly.
>
>   *
>
> I am reminded of a story
> Camus tells, of a man in prison camp.
>
> He had carved a piano keyboard
> with a nail on a piece of wood.
>
> And sat there playing the piano.
> This music was made entirely of silence.[1]

It may be that to write effective poems which address (even silently) something badly wrong in the outside world, you first have to ask yourself why you are writing them at all. Facing disaster, why compose that small frail thing, a poem? Why not throw down the pen, go really silent? 'In the midst of what is going on now,' wrote T.S. Eliot, writing *Little Gidding* in 1942 while bombs fell on London, 'it is hard when you sit down at a desk to feel that morning after morning spent fiddling with words and rhythms is a justified activity.'

During the violence in Northern Ireland, Seamus Heaney faced the same question. In an essay which goes to the heart of why and how a poet keeps writing when people are killing each other, he quotes Eliot's words and compares poems written in such times to Christ writing silently in the sand while dispersing a murderous crowd.[2]

In St John's Gospel, Christ says, 'Let him that is without sin among you, cast the first stone,' but at the same time writes something with his finger on the ground. Poetry, Heaney suggests, is like that silent writing.

> In one sense, the efficacy of poetry is nil – no lyric has ever stopped a tank. In another sense, it is unlimited. It is like the writing in the sand, in the face of which accusers and accused are left speechless and renewed.

Like the graffiti, the 'obscenities and hearts' in C.K. Williams's poem 'Tar', 'scribbled' on a day of nuclear accident, poetry is silent writing which 'holds our attention' in 'the rift between what is going to happen and whatever we would wish to happen'. A good poem works, Heaney says, 'as pure concentration, a focus where our power to concentrate is concentrated back on ourselves'. In the face of devastation, it can fortify readers, 'credit promptings of our intuitive being,' help us all say, 'in the shyest part of our nature, "Yes, I know something like that too. Yes, that's right."'[3]

If you think only of the politics, of sense, your poem will not work. It will lose its 'self-delighting inventiveness, its joy in being a process of language as well as a representation of things in the world.' Even under moral and political pressure, you have to put the music, the 'demands and promise of the artistic event', first. 'Poetry is its own reality.'[4]

On the other hand, poetry which ignores the horror outside completely, which is silent because it is shutting its eyes, is a caged bird. It risks seeming, and maybe it actually is, complicit. 'We listened to the canary's words,' wrote the Palestinian poet

Mahmoud Darwish in one of his last poems:

'Singing in a cage is possible
And so is happiness...'

Tomorrow, we will remember that we left the canary
In a cage, alone
Not singing to us
But to passing snipers.[5]

In any context, but above all a prison camp or Ramallah, what a good poem can do is help readers renew their own individuality. 'Faced with the brutality of the historical onslaught,' says Heaney, 'poems are practically useless. Yet they verify our singularity, they stake out the ore of self which lies at the base of every individuated life.'

That is why a question about inner life ends with a man playing silent music. We all need that silent piano to keep playing, that it may renew inner life in an outside world filled with snipers. But to say the unspeakable, poems have to find ways of saying that are not-saying, ways of not-telling which are also, like Viola's confession of love, a telling.

The politics, and tact about them, are inseparable from the music. So, since tone is a musical image, let's turn to music.

The first time John Cage mentioned the idea of a piece composed entirely of silence was in 1947, in a lecture. He said there should be a piece with no sounds in it. In 1948 he said he wanted to compose a piece of uninterrupted silence, 'and sell it to Muzak Co. It will be three or four and a half minutes in length, those being the standard lengths of "canned music", and its title will be Silent Prayer.'[6]

In the years before composing his 'silent piece', Cage came to feel there was no such thing as absence of sound. The difference between sound and what was called silence lay in the listener's switch of attention. 'The essential meaning of silence is the giving up of intention,' he said. Silence was the absence of intended sounds. It happened when you stopped being aware. 'Silence is not acoustic, it is a change of mind, a turning around.'[7]

In 1951, hoping to hear real silence, he visited an anechoic chamber but instead of hearing a real nothing he heard two sounds, his own nervous system and his circulating blood. That year he also saw the new white paintings by his friend Robert Rauschenberg. 'I responded immediately,' he said, 'not as objects, but as ways of seeing... You could say they were mirrors of the air.' He felt he must write his 'silent piece' now, or music would be 'lagging' behind painting.[8]

He was also studying Buddhism, and believed that the sounds of all things, animate and inanimate, 'should be honoured rather than enslaved'. Music had to be a process of discovery. Its job was to make us aware, without manipulation, of all sounds around us:

'An activity of sounds in which the artist found a way to let the sounds be themselves. And, in being themselves, to open the minds of people who made them, or listened to them, to other possibilities than they had previously considered.[9]

4'33'' (*Four Minutes, Thirty-Three Seconds*), finally composed in 1952, consisted of what the audience listened to in a silence filled with sounds of their environment. The pianist raised and lowered the keyboard lid to mark three movements. The audience heard a silent piano, trees rustling outside, rain on the roof, and in the third movement their own vexed mutterings – just as Cage in the anechoic chamber had heard sounds of his own body. Asked to attend to sound in a new way, they resented it fiercely. When the pianist got up to show the piece had ended, they burst into uproar.[10]

Rauschenberg had challenged normal ways of attending to paint, now Cage was challenging conventional ways of attending to sound.

Attention

The word which links the politics with the music, which Heaney uses in talking about poetry written in murderous moments of history and which Cage also used in talking about sound and silence, is attention.

This too involves tautness. 'Attention', like tone, is 'a stretching'. The word comes from Latin *tendere*, 'to stretch', and *attendere*, 'to stretch towards'. The music, the poem, is offered to the audience's tense attention.

We attend both to what is sounded, and to what is not. Cage asked his audience to attend to unintentional sound; a poem asks them to attend to implications, to things they supply in reponse.

Yesterday I mentioned C.K. Williams's poem 'Tar'. This poem is powered by anger – that human beings are at risk from their own technology and politicians lie about it. But the politics are mentioned directly in only two and a half out of thirty-five lines. Immediately after, the poet is watching the roofers again.

> we still know less than nothing: the utility company continues making
>   little of the accident,
> the slick federal spokesmen still have their evasions in some
>   semblance of order.
> Surely we suspect now we're being lied to, but in the meantime,
>   there are the roofers,
> setting winch-frames, sledging rounds of tar apart, and there I am,
>   on the curb across, gawking.[11]

The poem's tone is set by its focus on these roofers rather than the terrifying news. The poet says he is 'trying to distract myself', but the poem is not distracting its readers, rather asking them to attend to a moral question: why do we prefer to concentrate on smaller human things, obscenities, hearts, the danger of the roofers' work, rather than the mortal danger we are all in from our own technology?

Jessica in *The Merchant of Venice* says she is never merry when she hears sweet music and Lorenzo tells her that is because her 'spirits are attentive'. The quality of our attentiveness to a poem depends on our willingness to attend, but also on the poem's own quality of tension. Tension commands attention. Both speak to Number 1 of those meanings for 'tone'. Tone is the way your poem will hold attention. Through tension, it will achieve colour and pitch, make outward express inward, and keep all the different elements in play.

Paul Durcan exemplifies all four meanings of tone in his poem about poetic tension and torsion, 'A Spin in the Rain with Seamus Heaney'.

> You had to drive across to Donegal town
> To drop off a friend at the Dublin bus
> So I said I'd come along for the spin –
>
> A spin in the rain.
> Bales of rain
> But you did not alter your method of driving,

Which is to sit right down under the steering wheel
And to maintain an upwards-peering posture
Treating the road as part of the sky,

A method which motoring correspondents call
Horizontal-to-the-vertical.
The hills of Donegal put down their heads

As you circled upwards past their solitary farmhouses,
All those agèd couples drenched over firesides,
Who were once courting couples in parked cars.

You parked the car in Donegal town and we walked the shops –
Magee's Emporium and The Four Masters Bookshop.
You bought ice-cream cones. I bought women's magazines.

We drove on up through the hills past Mountcharles
And Bruckless and Ardara.
There was a traffic jam in Ardara,

Out of which you extricated yourself
With a jack-knife U-turn on a hairpin bend
With all the bashful panache of a cattle farmer –

A cattle farmer who is not an egotist
But who is a snail of magnanimity,
A verbal source of calm.
[...]

Standing with our backs to a deserted table-tennis table
We picked up a pair of table-tennis bats
And, without being particularly conscious of what we were at,

We began to bat the ball one to the other
Until a knock-up was in progress,
Holding our bats in pen grips.

So here we are playing a game of ping-pong
Which is a backdrop to our conversation
While our conversation is a backdrop to our game.
[...]

I could listen to you speak along these lines
For the rest of the day and I dare say
You could listen to me also speak along my lines:
[...]

I note that we are both of us
No mean strikers of the ball and that, although
We have different ways of addressing the table –

38

Myself standing back and leaping about,
Yourself standing close and scarcely moving –
What chiefly preoccupies us both is spin.
[…]
Poetry! To be able to look a bullet in the eye,
With a whiff of the bat to return it spinning to drop
Down scarcely over the lapped net; to stand still; to stop.[12]

At one level, this poem is about technical tension, a torsion which
it calls spin, and which the different poetic techniques exemplified
by these two poets have in common. Durcan is playing Heaney,
getting into Heaney's car, using a Heaneyesque form unlike most
of his own poems: three-liners of which two lines generally rhyme
or half-rhyme. There is a game going on, in which *spin* shifts
meaning from a car journey (Heaney driving) to technique in table-
tennis.

On the journey, the first meaning of *spin*, Heaney's driving
technique is 'to sit right down under, and maintain an upwards
peering posture / treating the road as part of the sky'. He gets out
of a traffic jam 'with a jack-knife U-turn on a hairpin bend'. He is
dexterous, but 'bashful' with it, 'not an egotist', and 'a verbal source
of calm': a typically tender Durcan appreciation of Heaney's poetic
persona, threaded with his own extravagancies ('bales of rain', 'snail
of magnanimity').

Then comes the game and spin's second meaning, the torsion
of words and lines on which 'poetry' and tone depend. The poets
are face to face now, not side by side: Durcan is tackling Heaney's
craft head on, with affectionate glances at his poems ('pen grips'
winks at Heaney's famous poem 'Digging') and the way Heaney
works by 'standing close and scarcely moving'. Durcan represents
himself as all over the place, 'standing back', 'leaping about'.

They have different techniques but what they share, 'what chiefly
preoccupies us', is 'spin'. They have 'different ways of addressing
the table' but are both 'no mean strikers of the ball'. They relax
tension in different ways (they bought different things into the
car, 'ice-cream cones', 'women's magazines'), but both are utterly
occupied with 'poetry'. Which means keeping their 'eye' on violence,
that 'bullet' which is part of the outside world (about which both
have written important poems), while focussing on the technique
('whiff of the bat', 'lapped net') summed up by 'spin'.

Hooked Atoms, Harmony, Holding Together

The reader's attention is unconscious as well as conscious because in the poem's tension there are notes we do not hear as well as those we do.

In music, when you bow a string on the violin or pluck one on a guitar, it vibrates and makes the air vibrate, so sound waves travel to our ears. But we do not hear that note alone. We also hear others, the octaves above that note, the thirds and the fifths, even though it sounds like hearing only one.

These unconsciously heard notes are the harmonics. They make up the acoustic body of every note. We would miss them if they weren't there but don't realise we are hearing them. In a sequence of notes, the harmonics vibrate together and go on vibrating throughout the tune. This is how words in a poem work too. Unheard harmonics buzz above and between all the words.

But words, unlike notes, hold unheard resonances of sense as well as sound. Some of their unheard resonances are the ideas and other words set going in every reader's responsive imagination, which power their whole relation with the poem.

These unheard resonances, however, depend on the individual reader and the baggage of knowledge and memory we each bring to the poem. We all have different associations to every word. Our response to the whole poem rises from our personal linkages, our conscious and unconscious associations, to the words. From our personal mesh of social, political, emotional and literary associations, particular words and ideas pop up, hook onto particular words in the poem, and emerge as understanding and insight.

Coleridge used these images of link and hook in explaining how words occur to you as you write a poem. In imagination, he said, 'impressions are linked together'. In each of us there are clusters of associations between words, ideas and images. 'Ideas, by having been together, acquire a power of recalling each other.' In one letter Coleridge speaks of 'the hooks and eyes of memory'.[13] The mathematician Henri Poincaré used the same image to describe inspiration in mathematics. New discoveries happen when different ideas combine in your mind and fuse, 'like the hooked atoms of Epicurus'.

Poincaré was writing around 1911, when atomist theory, having been dropped for two thousand years, was suddenly in the air again.

The early Greek atomists thought matter was made of indivisible things we cannot see, which move round and combine to make large objects we can see. Poincaré was quoting one of the earliest, Democritus, whose ideas Epicurus later developed.

Around 400 BC, Democritus suggested that atoms had different shapes and sizes. Some were concave, some convex, some rough. And some 'hook-shaped', which explained how they managed to combine.[14]

From atoms to words, from physics to poetry. George Steiner uses this same hooking image to describe how words in a poem silently suggest other words. Words in a poem, he says, are,

> in Coleridge's simile, 'hooked atoms', so construed as to mesh and cross-mesh with the greatest possible cluster of other words in the reticulations of the total body of the language.[15]

To both the composing poet and responding reader, a poem's words link up with other words, images and ideas already floating round in their minds. They also link up with other poems.

In any poetic tradition, new poems echo and answer old ones. Every new poem is resonant with old ones, every responsible poet is carrying on an unspoken dialogue with poems by other people. What happens when two poets face each other across a net is a distorted echo, like the 'ping' and 'pong' in Durcan's poem. Consciously or unconsciously, each poet responds to other voices, in their head, in their memory, which have nourished and keep on prompting and enriching their own.

But this happens with reading too. When we read a poem, its words resound for us with other words, images, rhythms, shapes and ideas from other poems we have read, which all contribute to our response.

This is one factor in reading which makes for differences between readers, and different readings of each poem.

But the musical resonances of words are somewhat different. They do not depend on other poems the reader remembers. They are part of the words' physicality. They also make up, perhaps, what Walt Whitman meant when he said there was 'a latent charm in words and in the voice ringing them'. Whitman felt the poet who caught and 'brought this out beyond all others' was Tennyson, one of the most musical poets in the business.

At the musical level, the important hooked atoms in a poem, the things which as we listen 'mesh and cross-mesh' (in Steiner's words) aurally, are its smallest particles, the syllables. We react to the patterning of syllables instinctively: even when we don't know the language we can hear sonic connections, repetitions and relationships. Every syllable has resonances, and it is the relationships between these resonances, the ways *they* hook up, which makes words feel good together and create the poem's harmony. 'The syllable, that fine creature,' said Charles Olson, 'leads the harmony on.' [16]

'Harmony' comes from Greek *harmottein*, 'to join, to fit together'. The musical meaning of *harmonia* in ancient Greece was a type of tuning, a 'mode' which related the musical tones in its own way. Different *harmonias* carried different moral and emotional weight. Tuning them depended on tension, stretching skin over a drum, strings on the lyre. The underlying image of *harmottein* is carpentry: pegs 'fitting into' the lyre, strings tied to wood.

But in *harmonia* it is also different voices 'joining' each other. Harmony reminds us of Number 4 above, the tone that is a balance of different elements. *Harmonia* is all about relation. In ancient Athens, music was an image of all civilisedness. Solon, the Athenian law-giver, called the Muses the 'key to the good life'. *Mousa* meant a song or poem (to 'carry a *mousa*' was 'to sing a song') but also the personified source of everything implied by *mousike*, the adjective meaning 'musical.' No one bothered to add the missing noun *techne*, 'art' or 'skill', to *mousike*. You had to understand it. *Mousike* meant knowledge of other civilising arts, not only music: any art over which the Muses presided.

There were originally (people said) three Muses, Song, Practice and Memory. Later on, there were nine. They were the sources of, respectively, epic, lyric, tragedy, comedy, choral poetry and dance, and also history and astronomy, which were more linked to poetry than we might think. The historian Herodotus, whose main medium of delivery was public recitation, named each of the nine books of his *Histories* after a different Muse. The first Greek book on astronomy, by Thales, was in Homer's metre, dactylic hexameter.

So a *mousikos* was an 'educated, cultured' person, and philosophers and medical writers use *harmonia* as image of unity, balance and order, whether social, physical or cosmic. Well-run relations between men and gods, or husbands and wives, are *harmonia*. In the state, *harmonia* is political order, 'weak and strong citizens blending their voices to sing the same thing'. In the body but also the soul (which Plato said was 'held together by tensions and opposites'), *harmonia* was the balance of different elements.[17]

Harmonia is order created concentrically, by the power of drawing together which is the centre of Orpheus's art. In *The Merchant of Venice*, Lorenzo pictures Orpheus calming violent nature, animate and inanimate, by magnetising all creatures towards his music.

> Do but note a wild and wanton herd,
> Or race of youthful and unhandled colts,
> Fetching mad bounds, bellowing and neighing loud,
> Which is the hot condition of their blood;
> If they but hear perchance a trumpet sound,
> Or any air of music touch their ears,
> You shall perceive them make a mutual stand,
> Their savage eyes turn'd to a modest gaze
> By the sweet power of music: therefore the poet
> Did feign that Orpheus drew trees, stones, and floods;
> Since nought so stockish, hard, and full of rage,
> But music for the time doth change his nature.[18]

Like 'tone' and 'attention', *harmonia* involves tension. The elements it combines, the wild colts, are violent. One slip and discord is back. Losing *harmonia* means violence in the city, disease in the body, anguish in the soul. Orpheus therefore ends up torn apart, dismembered by maenads. His voice lived on but the Muses (whose dances are image of the united, the concentric) gathered up the pieces of his body and buried them.

Harmonia, however, is a mythical personage as well as a concept. And as a character too she is unitedness surrounded by destruction.

Her parents are Aphrodite, goddess of love, personification of joining, and Ares god of war, personification of destruction. When she marries, the Muses dance at her wedding and her wedding gift is a golden necklace which, like a jewel with a curse on it, creates havoc among who wear, desire and steal it, causing treachery between family members, the destruction of palaces and cities. Yet one poet calls Harmonia the mother of the Muses.

Everything about *harmonia*, as concept, political metaphor or musical term, embodied in Orpheus or personified by Harmonia, speaks of tension between calm joining and tearing apart. No wonder a word which lets the tone down scuppers a poem's chances in a competition. *Harmonia* exists on a knife edge. One fraction out of balance and you're lost. Harmony is the still eye of the typhoon. The poem has to, in Durcan's words, 'be able to look a bullet in the eye' and then return that bullet 'spinning', make it 'drop down scarcely over the lapped net; to stand still, to stop'. Poetry, like harmony, is a dangerous business.

Syllables and Silent Letters

Language requires harmony and Harmonia's husband Cadmus was the hero credited with teaching the secrets of speech. He did it by combining consonants with vowels.

'Consonant' comes from Latin *con-sonare*, 'to sound with'. Because consonants cannot be syllables on their own. Some look as if they can, like the L in table, but need a silent vowel to help them.

Consonants differentiate. They make edges, like the cement "pointing" bricks in a wall. They are sounds in which air-flow is stopped by the tongue, glottis or lips. In Hebrew, the world's oldest recorded and still spoken language, the word for consonant is *atsur*, which means 'closed' or 'stopped'. Consonants stop the breath. They define syllables but do not make a word move forward.

In vowels, the vocal tract is open. No build-up of air pressure above the glottis, no closure of throat or mouth. 'Vowel' comes from *vocalis*, Latin for 'speaking'. Vowels are the nucleus of the syllable. You need a vowel to *say* a syllable.

You also need breath. In speaking a poem, as in singing, breath is the fundamental. In singing, what you pitch and hold are vowels. The only consonants you can sing are those which sometimes act as vowels, like Y, or the liquid consonants L, M, N, R. Otherwise, you don't pitch a consonant, you articulate it. Consonants mark one sung note off from the next, because they stop the breath. You sing what you use the breath for, vowels. They are the movement of a word. Hebrew's word for vowel, *tenu'ah*, means 'movement'. It is an anapoest – tenu' ă – and even its shape, with the accent on accent on the last syllable, enacts a forward movement.

Poetry itself is movement and in any language poems live off the vowel sounds. Long and short, stressed and unstressed, vowels are the movement as well as the inner music of a poem.

But what happens when all these sounds, vowel and consonant and the larger sounds they make which we call words, are written down? Writing is itself a silencing. The sound has gone. In its place are signs.

Different languages and alphabets create their own relationship between sounds and their written signs. Both in our alphabets and the spelling that results from them, and in the way we talk and relate to each other, we take the silences of our own conventions for granted. But different conventions, operating in other languages and societies, may tell us something more generally what letters are doing when they represent sounds in a poem.

Semitic alphabets, like Phoenician, Arabic and Hebrew, are consonantal alphabets, now known as *abjads*. They do not have vowels. In Hebrew, for instance, *aleph* and *ayin* are guttural sounds. *Ayin* is a consonant which represents a guttural silence, a glottal stop. The structure of Semitic languages meant you did not need to mark the vowels. The words are formed from a root of (usually three) consonants. The vowel sounds emerge in inflected forms of the root.

When the Greeks started to develop writing, they adapted the Phoenician script, but the phonetic structure of Greek was very different from Phoenician and meaning became too ambiguous if they did not represent the vowels too. Since Greek did not need letters for the guttural sounds represented by *aleph* or *ayin*, they gave those symbols vowel values instead. So Greek became the first alphabet to include vowels. *Alpha* was born.

Hebrew, for a long time, did not mark the vowels at all. In reading a text, the reader supplied the relevant vowel, as we do today in text messaging. Later on, Arabic and Hebrew both developed vowel marks (*nikkud* for Hebrew, *harakāt* in Arabic): dots below or near the consonant which indicated the spoken vowel. You don't have to use them, practised readers don't. Hebrew poetry, however, always marks the vowels.

Theoretically, non-Semitic languages could also be written without vowels. Many European languages would lose grammatical information like gender or number, but English would be easier. There are even poems these days in text message form.

The relationship between written and spoken sound, the idea

of leaving out in text a sound you say when speaking, brings us to the concept of silent letters. These are letters which are present but not pronounced in any particular word.

At one level, silent letters come about because of the word's origins. 'Vineyard' is pronounced *vinyard*: the silent E shows you the origin of the word in 'vine'. But more deeply, you could say that silent letters are born out of the gulf between speaking and writing.

Silent letters make problems for people who don't know the language, because it is hard to guess the spelling. Newly developed alphabets for previously unwritten languages don't have them, nor do planned languages like Esperanto.

English, however, perhaps because the language comes from so many linguistic sources, so many complicated grammars, has far more than its fair share. The consonants which go silent in English are B, C, D, G, GH, H, K, L, N, P, S, T and W.[19] As for vowels – U can be silent after G and before a vowel, as in guitar, but above all our silent E at the end of words lengthens an inner vowel.

We don't think about the silent letters in our own systems. The ones we notice are those in someone else's, when we try and learn another language. We take our own silences for granted. They are a useful image for everything we do not notice we are hearing in a poem; for all the silences in and around its words.

Poetry is concentrated language. Its job is to combine vowels, consonants and silence in harmony. Its essential unit is the syllable, which Charles Olson calls 'the king and pin of versification' because it 'holds together the lines, the even larger forms, of a poem'. It is the syllables, little combinations of vowel and consonant, which hum with unheard resonances. A poem's harmony depends on how its syllables hang together.

'Syllable' comes from *sullambanein*, 'to grasp or hold together'. The Greek *sullabe*, something which holds or is held together, can mean a 'hold' in wrestling, the 'fastening' of a girdle, or a single sound which holds together those different letters, consonants and vowels.

What letters are in a syllable, so words are in a poem. The crucial thing, *harmonia*, holds all the elements together. Poems, like syllables, need containing. And containing is the main image through which Emily Dickinson compares the relation between syllable and sound to that between our consciousness and the world.

The containers here are 'brain', 'sponges', 'buckets' and the 'sound' which holds the syllables together. But the poem too is a container, a small thing which contains all these sounds but also the dizzyingly large ideas.

> The Brain – is wider than the Sky –
> For – put them side by side –
> The one the other will contain
> With ease – and You – beside –
>
> The Brain is deeper than the sea –
> For – hold them – Blue to Blue –
> The one the other will absorb –
> As Sponges – Buckets – do –
>
> The Brain is just the weight of God –
> For – Heft them – Pound for Pound –
> And they will differ – if they do –
> As Syllable from Sound – [20]

Emily is having fun. Syllables *are* the sound. And the neatest way of relating one syllable to another, at least in English, is the instrument which contains this poem and makes it hang together by framing the unmatched words ('God', 'syllable') with ones that match: 'brain'/'contain', 'blue'/'You do'/'do', 'sea'/'ease', 'pound'/ 'sound'. In an English-language poem, the most telling way of relating different elements, the supreme instrument of harmony, is rhyme.

Echo and the Poetry of Relation

Rhymes are the essential unsounded harmonics which syllables carry with them as they move through a poem. Just as harmonics of musical notes blend together unheard above tunes and chords, so unspoken rhymes hum round the words of a poem as you read, affecting how you respond to the whole.

Let's take an extended example from that master of music, Tennyson. The passage I want to look at comes near the end of a long poem, but he is so musically connective that we have to look at the beginning and end first.

His poem 'Tithonus' is spoken by the man who cannot die. He lives with the goddess of the dawn. She fell in love with him when he was young and gave him immortality but forgot to stop him ageing, so he staggers on decrepit while she remains dewy young.

The poem (I have italicised words and syllables I want to pick out) begins with things which do what Tithonus cannot. Die. 'Fall' – down to earth.

> The woods decay, the woods decay and fall,
> The vapours weep their burthen to the ground,
> Man comes and tills the field and lies beneath,
> And after many a summer dies the swan.
> Me only cruel immortality
> Consumes; I wither slowly in thine arms,
> Here at the quiet limit of the world,
> A white-hair'd shadow *roaming* like a dream
> The ever-silent spaces of the East,
> Far-folded mists, and *gleaming* halls of morn.

At the very end, Tithonus begs the dawn to let him die:

> Release me, and restore me to the ground;
> Thou seest all things, thou wilt see my grave:
> Thou wilt renew thy beauty morn by morn;
> I earth in earth forget these empty courts,
> And thee *returning* on thy silver wheels.

The passage I want to focus on is the penultimate movement. It begins with 'me' and ends with the birth of another thing scheduled to die: Troy, *Ilion*, the city built by Apollo's music, whose fall is the West's first great metaphor for doomed civilisation.

> Ay me! ay me! with what another heart
> In days far-off, and with what other eyes
> I used to watch – if I be he that watched –
> The lucid outline *forming* round thee; saw
> The *dim* curls *kin*dle into sunny *rings*;
> Changed with thy mystic change, and felt my blood
> Glow with the glow that slowly *crim*soned all
> Thy presence and thy portals, while I lay,

Mouth, forehead, eyelids, *growing* dewy-warm
With kisses balmier than half-*opening* buds
Of April, and could hear the lips that kissed
Whispering I knew not what of wild and sweet,
Like that strange song I heard Apollo *sing*,
While Ilion like a mist rose into towers.

'Sing' is the generative climax (Apollo's song created Troy), prepared for by 'dim', 'kindle', 'rings', 'crimson' and the present participles ('forming', 'growing', 'opening', 'whispering') which follow 'roaming' and 'gleaming' at the beginning, and are picked up in the last line by 'returning'.

These participles show Tithonus surrounded by tragically uncompleted change. For normal people, present participles have a proper end: ageing and dying lead to death. But his lover keeps 'returning' to her first freshness.

This passage shows her renewing herself, both through 'dim' to 'kindle' and 'crimson', and through participles which create an image of inexorably soft self-refreshing. Through this apparently 'blank' verse, the *–ing* sounds set up in us one particular unsounded rhyme, an unspoken word which reminds us of who and what Tithonus's lover really is. She is the everlasting beginning, young like the beginning of their love, as 'buds of April'. She is the beginning of day. She is eternal 'spring'. A word which also means 'leap up', the opposite of what Tithonus has longed to do from the first line's 'fall'. And also means source of both fresh water and, mythologically, of poetic inspiration. Semantically, 'spring' sums up all she is, and everything he has lost the power to do or be. Musically, we feel it coming at us from all those *–ing* words. It is their unsounded echo.

Echo, a sound darting from yourself to somewhere else and back, is essential to poetry. 'Echo poems' from the sixteenth and seventeenth centuries play with the end word's harmonics: they follow each line, a statement or question, with a new word which echoes its last syllable or syllables. The reflected sound supposedly comes from Nature or divinity, but it is prompted by a human question.

George Herbert's echo poem 'Heaven' is an image of communication with God. The echo is divine counsel made of human language, and answers the mortal questions by re-sounding them.

O who will show me those delights on high?
        Echo.   I.
Thou Echo, thou art mortall, all men know.
        Echo.   No.
Wert thou not born among the trees and leaves?
        Echo.   Leaves.
And are there any leaves, that still abide?
        Echo.   Bide.
What leaves are they? impart the matter wholly.
        Echo.   Holy.
Are holy leaves the Echo then of blisse?
        Echo.   Yes.
Then tell me, what is that supreme delight?
        Echo.   Light.
Light to the minde: what shall the will enjoy?
        Echo.   Joy.
But are there cares and businesse with the pleasure?
        Echo.   Leisure.
Light, joy, and leisure; but shall they persever?
        Echo.   Ever.

The answer lies in rhyme. But does it come from inside or outside the questioner?

The sound of another mind echoing ours is the 'fantasy of intimacy', as one critic has called it, also in relations between readers and poems. The poem, someone else's voice, can feel like a distorted version of our own.[21] Keats says in a letter that a poem 'should strike the Reader as a wording of his own highest thoughts and almost as a Remembrance'.

At the end of the balcony scene, Juliet cannot bear to let Romeo go. She cannot shout, her father's guards would hear and kill him, so she calls him back in a whisper –

Else would I tear the cave where Echo lies
And make her airy tongue more hoarse than mine
With repetition of my Romeo's name. Romeo!

Romeo comes back to her with that fantasy of intimacy, the feeling that the other's voice is yours, that your inwardness is inside them. 'It is my soul that calls upon my name.'[22]

But what echo gets up to in Herbert's poem also suggests the relationship between the poet and the words. These words seem to be yours, but they often feel as if they come from outside. As if what is deep and unconscious in you, the well of memory and imagination where Coleridge and Poincaré picture words and ideas hooking onto each other, rising to the surface, is actually outside you. As if the words come from somewhere else entirely.

Poets often feel a poem comes to them from outside, and Echo is one of Wordsworth's main metaphors for voice. Echo is both yours and not yours, a voice from inside and outside. She relates inside to outside, question to answer. Echo offers an image of relating in which you know it is your own power which starts things off, and yet you can wonder at the voice as if it belonged to someone else.

Seamus Heaney suggests that it is when a poet becomes 'classic-ally empowered' that he or she discovers 'the poetry of relation'. He illustrates this idea with Wordsworth's 'There was a boy, which Wordsworth later incorporated into his *Prelude*. The boy calls to owls and hears their calls (and echoes of them) coming back to him.

> ...with fingers interwoven, both hands
> Pressed closely palm to palm and to his mouth
> Uplifted, he, as through an instrument,
> Blew mimic hootings to the silent owls
>   That they might answer him. And they would shout
> Across the watery vale, and shout again,
> Responsive to his call, with quivering peals,
> And long halloos, and screams, and echoes loud
> Redoubled and redoubled; concourse wild
> Of jocund din! [23]

The owls were 'silent', the boy hoped 'they might answer him', and they became 'responsive'. Poetic empowering is an answer, a voice, a sound responding to sounds which you have made.

Heaney's poem 'Personal Helicon' embodies this empowering through relation. It begins with the poet remembering a childhood fascination with wells, and any deep darkness from which water was brought up. Some wells created their own sound:

> One, in a brickyard, with a rotted board top.
> I savoured the rich crash when a bucket
> Plummeted down at the end of a rope.

Others, when he called down them, 'had echoes, gave back your own call / with a clean new music in it'. In one, 'a white face hovered over the bottom'. The poem ends with the adult poet not peering

in wells but writing poems instead. Which, since he is dealing with
echo, he calls rhyme.

> Now, to pry into roots, to finger slime,
> To stare, big-eyed Narcissus, into some spring
> Is beneath all adult dignity. I rhyme
> To see myself, to set the darkness echoing.

'Slime', the word he rhymes with 'rhyme', recalls the foulness
where Yeats finds poetry in his poem 'The Circus Animals' Deser-
tion'. Not in the glamorous mythic images he used to use, which
anyway grew ultimately out of something pretty similar to Heaney's
brickyard and rotted boards:

> A mound of refuse or the sweepings of a street,
> Old kettles, old bottles, and a broken can,
> Old iron, old bones...

Instead of the exotica, says Yeats, 'I must be satisfied with my
heart.' Where he finds poetry now is in 'the foul rag and bone
shop' of the self.

Heaney's poem locates the source of poetry in a quest 'to see
myself'. But it also points to the classical 'source' of poetry, Heli-
con, the Greek mountain sacred to the Muses where the Hippocrene
spring, image of poetic inspiration (like the 'new music' brought
up from Heaney's wells), gushed out when their winged horse
Pegasus struck his hoof on a rock.

Heaney's phrase 'the poetry of relation' sums up much of what
tone is and does. The taut holding together, of Muses in their
dance, of letters in a syllable, sounds in a poem. But also the rela-
tion between words and poet, reader and poem. the relating is
musical and personal, both at once. In these last three poems you
see the poet, Wordsworth, Yeats and Heaney, being empowered
through relationship with four sorts of thing.

One, the world outside. Wordsworth's and Heaney's poems revel
in the world's physicality, the 'watery vale', the roots around wells.
'I loved,' says Heaney, 'the dark drop, the trapped sky, the smells /
Of waterweed, fungus and dank moss.'

Secondly, myth and stories. The beautiful images which Yeats
calls 'circus animals'. Figures of Greek myth like Heaney's Narcissus.

Thirdly, other people's poems. For Heaney, of course, Words-
worth and Yeats.

Finally, supremely, yourself. Wordsworth's boy has 'fingers interwoven', hands pressed closely palm to palm. 'Seeing myself' in Heaney's poem is also setting 'the darkness echoing', a darkness which is both inside you and outside.

This is where Echo as mythic personage comes in, the nymph who fell in love (also, as it happens, on Mount Helicon) with the boy who fell in love with himself.

According to one story, Echo was a nymph with a lovely voice who refused all male advances. When she spurned the god Pan, he made his followers tear her into pieces, like Orpheus. These were scattered over Earth. As the Muses gathered the torn limbs of Orpheus, so Earth collected Echo's limbs. But not her voice. This lived on, like that of Orpheus and lingers still in all the world's hollow places, repeating the last word other people say.

In another story, Echo was a nymph with a beautiful voice, who loved the sound of her own voice. She distracted the goddess Hera, while Hera's husband went off after other nymphs, by her talk. When Hera realised she punished Echo by taking away all her voice except the power of repeating someone else's words.

Originally, these stories were separate from that of Narcissus but the Roman poet Ovid saw resemblances between the two figures and brilliantly connected them. The version he set going is Echo's third story.

Narcissus is a gorgeous young hunter who spurns all would-be lovers, including Echo. Perhaps because he rejects everyone anyway or perhaps because all she can do is repeat his words. Echo wastes away, pining for a love she never knew. Narcissus is punished for her sorrow by falling in love with himself in a forest pool. He too wastes away for love, and Echo mourns him from her lonely cave.

Echo inhabits a hollow dark like our own unconscious. John Cage's anechoic chamber was a silence filled with the sounds of self. Echo's cave is the empty darkness you self-empoweringly fill with your own voice – or is there someone really there, an attentive and adoring presence?

In echo poems, Echo tells divine truth. That phrase of Juliet's, 'the cave where Echo lies' suggests that the sound of self may not always tell the truth. She may lie. But too bad she is all poets have to work with.

In Heaney's 'Helicon', the word that rhymes with 'echoing' describes what he sees himself in: the 'spring', the word unspoken in 'Tithonus'. Male Western poetry is still empowered by the way Greek thought personified human experience and concepts (like Harmonia) as female. The Muse is a live empowering force for male poets still: a voice from outside and inside, a source (like Helicon's spring) of knowledge you did not know you had. Echo too is empowering. She is an 'acoustic mirror' like female voices in many films. She is the shadow Muse who met Narcissus on the Muses' mountain.

It was just accident, surely, but a lucky one for that ikon of male creativity Bob Dylan (who went on to write 'My Love, She Speaks like Silence' to the woman he married) that the first name of Miss Helstrom, his first high-school girlfriend, was Echo.[24]

'I rhyme to see myself.' Echo, the voice from the dark, the rhyme that comes to you from outside or inside or both, is inspiration and empowerment. Myself and not.

That, perhaps, is why rhyme is such an emotive issue.

The Viola Voice: Making Music With

'Heard melodies are sweet, but those unheard are sweeter,' says Keats to the Greek vase, the 'silent form' which he calls a 'bride of quietness' and 'foster-child of Silence'. But there are different sorts of unheard melody. Another musical parallel to sounds unheard in a poem are the inner notes of chords. Come in the viola, middle member of the violin family.

The viola has not the brilliance of a violin or power of the cello. You hold it under the chin like a violin but it is bigger and lower. It has the same strings as a cello but is an octave higher and much smaller. Viola is inside and covert, the supporter, the harmoniser, smoky and muted beside the flash of the fiddle, softer than the rich baritone of a cello.

In the orchestra you hear violins on top, and the cello, male to the fiddle's female, dark to violin radiance, beneath. The viola is between. In a string quartet, a viola intermittently answers both violin and cello. It is the inner voice, the answerer from the shadows.

Like Echo in her cave, the viola voice is within. It needs to be

there, but is often unattended to. Many listeners hear it without
realising, like shadows they are unaware of seeing in a painting.
You often have to work to hear it – like the *dark* voice which
finally comes to the poet in a poem by James Wright, 'Depressed
by a Book of Bad Poetry, I Walk Toward an Unused Pasture and
Invite the Insects to Join Me'.

At this point the poet has dropped the book of bad poetry and
is walking slightly upward, as if on Mount Helicon, in search of
new sounds, or maybe of ground as yet untrodden by poems and
poets. Though that pasture he walks towards may be an ironic
echo of the last line of Milton's 'Lycidas', 'Tomorrow to fresh
fields and pastures new'.

> I climb a slight rise of grass.
> I do not want to disturb the ants
> Who are walking single file up the fence post,
> Carrying small white petals,
> Casting shadows so frail I can see through them.
> I close my eyes for a moment, and listen.
> The old grasshoppers
> Are tired, they leap heavily now,
> Their thighs are burdened.
> I want to hear them, they have clear sounds to make.
> Then lovely, far off, a dark cricket begins
> In the maple trees.[25]

Cage would approve. Looking for a new sound for his own voice,
Wright's poet turns his attention to what normally goes unnoticed,
the smallest visible life-forms, the sounds of apparent silence.

He notices invertebrates. At first he sees what they carry, which
cast shadows 'so frail I can see through them'. Then he closes off
seeing and concentrates entirely on hearing. At first he hears 'clear
sounds' sung by 'old grasshoppers'. Old ways of making poems,
perhaps. But then a new sound arrives, a voice from the trees.

This is 'lovely', 'dark' and also distant, echoing the famous line
'lovely, dark and deep' describing woods in Robert Frost's poem
'Stopping by Woods on a Snowy Evening'. In Frost's poem, the
poet listens to snow falling on trees. It is not silence, not entirely.
The horse is jingling its harness and

> The only other sound's the sweep
> Of easy wind and downy flake.

Just as Cage's silence is full of sounds we do not normally attend to, so the 'unused pasture' of Wright's poem is full of echoes from older poems. The new thing, the dark cricket hidden in the trees, is invisible as Echo in her cave or the viola's dusky voice within the chord.

The viola's job is relating. It is the inside of harmony. It evolved as an inner voice, so it is hard for a viola to be heard above an orchestra, but perversely, from the Baroque era onwards, composers tried to get it to. Telemann and Stamitz wrote viola concertos. Bach's *6th Brandenburg Concerto* does away with violins and makes the violas the top voice. In the 1830s, after the Romantics had been highlighting inner self in many different art forms, Berlioz wrote *Harold in Italy*. 'I wanted,' he said, 'to make the viola a melancholy dreamer in the manner of Byron's Childe-Harold.' His solo viola represents Byron's dark, dramatic, self-doubting romantic hero. The self-obsessed 20th century added more viola concertos by Bartok and Walton, and Britten's unaccompanied viola piece *Lacrimae*, and Morton Feldman's 1970 chamber piece entitled *The Viola in My Life*.

But the composer who most showed the world how to love the viola was Mozart, that relator of genius. He wrote wonderful viola parts in chamber music, and in his *Sinfonia Concertante* he does have a solo viola. But this is partnered by a solo violin. It is a double concerto. Solo violin and viola, as passionate as any pair of lovers stand alone against the orchestra like Tony and Maria in *West Side Story* meeting on the dark stage as other people dance around them.

The viola's innerness has made it the instrument of choice for composers because playing the viola is the best place to hear all the notes. J.S. Bach's son said his father always heard 'the slightest wrong note in even the largest combination', and 'As the greatest expert and judge of harmony, he liked best to play the viola'. So did Haydn, Mozart, Schubert, Dvorak, Beethoven, Mendelssohn, Britten, Frank Bridge, Hindemith, Vaughan Williams. Even Jimi Hendrix, according to a leaflet for a Hendrix CD, *Jimi Hendrix: The Ultimate Collection*, began his musical career on the viola.

But Mozart is the one who shows us how the ideal harmonising voice is never inert. It answers and moves with the others and occasionally, when the music demands, comes out from its cave in a brief solo. The viola is the ultimate musical instrument because *harmonia* is about relationship and the viola stands for making music *with*. The viola voice is the harmony at the heart of the poetry of relation.

Like a symphony (from *symphonon*, something 'sounding together'), a poem's sound is made of relationships between many different voices. You might compare the viola concerto to 20th-century confessional poetry. The viola evolved not to *need* limelight: to be inside and surface occasionally. And many "personal" poems do not sound the confessional note all the time. C.K. Williams' poem 'Tar' is very personal, but it focusses on the roofers. What the 'I' does and feels comes in as an aside.

The viola, buried in the harmony as Wright's dark cricket is hidden in the maples, is the perfect image for energies lurking in the harmony of even the smallest poem, which we may not on first reading notice that we hear. But in among the words of most good poems are many different forms of life to which we unwittingly react. Among them, the registers.

Register: Talking and Talking Back

Register is another musical term. It too reminds us that what goes on in a poem emotionally is also part of its sound. 'Register' originally meant a 'rank' of pipes on the organ. Today in music it means the range (or part of the range) of any instrument or human voice.

Register, like harmony, echo and the viola, is about relation. It refers to related notes in the same range. But it is also about pitch. Violins play in a higher register than cellos. So when you say that a single note is in a particular register, what you are doing is relating it to the other notes in that range.

In ordinary speech, we use the verb 'to register' in two ways. To mean 'show a feeling in your face' ('His face should have registered horror') but also to refer to something entering your consciousness, a moment of realisation. ('The sound of breaking glass did not register.') The relating that this verb points to is a relating (like Echo) of inside and outside. Something affecting your consciousness comes in from outside. Or something comes out from inside you, to be expressed on your surface.

So how about register in poems?

This too is about something coming out from inside – voice. But voice in poems is not straightforward. The poem itself is the only clue to the speaker and the situation.

If the poem says 'I', this does not necessarily mean the poet. (Another reason for the news editor I mentioned yesterday to be suspicious.) A poem's 'I' is a speaker for whom every word builds an implied identity.

The voice of poems that have no 'I' also comes from an implied speaker, whose situation the poem hints at as it goes. This voice can be a hard thing for a poet to find. 'The thing is,' W.S. Graham said once in a letter, 'to find or create (in this case the same thing) a language, a timbre of thought or voice.' [26] John Ashbery, in his *Robert Frost Medal Address*, described how he changed his style by leafing 'through popular magazines, looking for the tone of voice I thought was lacking'.

A poem creates its voice by the registers it uses. Register, like a code, *positions* the speaker. Language is an activity of people in situations and poetry uses ordinary speech. A poem talks – but it also plays with talking. How poems frame and re-position the talking they do is by changing register.

In linguistics, a register is a socially recognisable range of related sounds, a style of language used in a particular setting. The same person may use perfect grammar in a formal meeting (no 'ain't', for instance), but speak quite differently in the pub. You use different tones of voice to address a small child, a footballer who has just missed a penalty, your partner, and the person in the BT call centre guiding you through horrors on your computer.

In a poem, register suggests a social situation. It sends messages about who is talking, to whom, and why. But this is social situation framed and on show. Register in a poem is language put on show for a purpose. It can be colloquial, intimate, formal, gentle, ruthless. It is determined by what is happening, who is taking part, what role the language is playing. Because register is part of social exchange, listeners react very differently to different registers.

Good poems manipulate registers (and therefore the reader's feelings about all the words) just as organists manipulate the ranks of organ pipes.

If you want a consistent register, you select one range, pulling out the stop on one particular rank of pipes. But most good poems combine several registers. How poets shift register is a crucial aspect of their voice. Some poems shift register on one word and back on the next with a twist of perspective like the *spin* in Durcan's poem when the bullet flicks over the net. One register may let the voice inhabit the words fully, but another will interrogate the way it presents them.

By creating a new register, the poem can wink at or undermine words it has just used. Philip Larkin once described Ian Hamilton telling him that whenever he said anything in a poem, 'I give a little twist to show I didn't mean it.'

Register is slippery, like the tuning pegs on a violin. It is where a poet can bring together all voices of a culture, all resources of the language. The agility of the language, how alive it is, depends on the ways the registers combine.

In Selima Hill's poem 'A Small Hotel', the registers are disconnected from each other. A different one turns up in each couplet.

My nipples tick
like little bombs of blood.

Someone is walking
in the yard outside.

I don't know why
Our Lord was crucified.

A really good fuck
makes me feel like custard.[27]

The speaker begins and ends by talking about her own body, but the title and inner couplets imply a dramatic situation. Rhymes link the two inner couplets ('outside'/'crucified'), and the two outer ones ('blood'/'custard'), giving the poem the concentric unity of *harmonia*. But the couplets themselves, each in a different register, are disconnected, like the dismembered bodies of Orpheus or Echo. They do not merge as you read. Each new couplet and register suggests new emotional information about the speaker and her situation. Is this an adulterous couple? Do 'tick' and 'bombs' in the first couplet suggest they are about to be discovered? The second couplet seems simply descriptive, but is there anxiety about who the 'someone outside' is? The leap of reference in the third, and Our Lord, position the speaker as a frightened or disturbed Catholic, thinking of violence. The violence in the fourth couplet is only a

'really good fuck'. Yet the unexpected register of these lines, itali-
cised to mark their difference, changes the tone of the whole poem.

Jo Shapcott's poem 'The Mad Cow Talks Back' gives us anoth-
er speaker talking about her body. But here, in a stanza-less block
poem, the different registers shift fluidly into each other.

> I'm not mad. It just seems that way
> because I stagger and get a bit irritable.
> There are wonderful holes in my brain
> through which ideas from outside can travel
> at top speed and through which voices,
> sometimes whole people, speak to me
> about the universe. Most brains are too
> compressed. You need this spongy
> generosity to let the others in.
>
> I love the staggers. Suddenly the surface
> of the world is ice and I'm a magnificent
> skater turning and spinning across whole hard
> Pacifics and Atlantics. It's risky when
> you're good, so of course the legs go before,
> behind, and to the side of the body from time
> to time, and then there's the general embarrassing
> collapse, but when that happens it's glorious
> because it's always when you're travelling
> most furiously in your mind. My brain's like
> the hive: constant little murmurs from its cells
> saying this is the way, this is the way to go.[28]

This poem was written at the height of 'mad cow disease' when
British television was showing staggery cows every night on the
news. The registers change as it goes, now colloquial ('top speed',
'the general embarrassing collapse'), now visionary ('a magnificent /
skater'... 'spinning across whole hard Pacifics and Atlantics'), now
confidential ('you need'; 'it just seems that way'), now confident
and excited ('wonderful', 'magnificent', 'glorious').

These registers are multiple, in fact, as the *holes* (laughingly
picked up in 'whole people', 'whole Pacifics') riddling her brain.
They are also as slippery as the surface she spins on, destabilising
the reader to match her own staggers and making her a thoroughly
unreliable narrator of herself.

Even the title seems to be in two registers, as if the word 'mad'
is both the poem's own and someone else's, both mocking and self-

mocking: as if whoever is saying it has been called 'mad cow' by someone else and is 'talking back' through the persona of a cow with BSE.

The lunatic merging of different kinds of thing ('spongy generosity', 'hard Pacifics and Atlantics') questions the denial of madness at the outset. And yet, through all the jokes, the mix reminds us that visionaries often are called mad.

The ways these two poems manage their shifts of register is part of the world view of each poem but also reflects the voice and preoccupations of each poet across their whole oeuvre. Hill uses juxtaposition and wild leaps of imagery to evoke narratives of the unconscious. Her voice is surreal and symbolic, pivoting on images in quick transition. It feels flamboyant, but the registers are utterly disciplined. Their separation from each other contributes to the sense which emanates from Hill's voice of a speaker existing in a world of disconnected fragments. In Shapcott's poem, the way the registers merge into each other reflects the way the voice challenges the separateness of self and other. 'What interests me most,' she has said, 'is the exact place where the self and the other touch.' Many of her poems ('Quark', for instance) are both a talking and a talking *back*.

In this one, who is calling this cow mad? Is the title part of what the speaker is saying, is she repeating it ironically? Or is it someone else's way of describing this poem? Who is being seen and heard and by whom? Subject and object merge.

The way a poet combines registers is part of how you recognise them. Poets find different ways to shift register. They do it through wit and humour, making new words laugh at earlier ones. Or through metaphor, which, as we saw yesterday, bounces us into a new way of looking at things. Or through parenthesis, irony, self-correction. Or through direct and indirect speech, as in Anne Sexton's poem 'Red Roses'.[29]

This poem involves a relationship. Not just a speaker and her body but a mother and child. The situation created through the swivelling registers involves pretence, so the shifts in register are more complicated, and sometimes disingenuous. The poem is structured in three continuous movements followed by a separated coda. Each movement closes with lines in an apparently factual comment register, which sum up the new information.

Tommy is three and when he's bad
his mother dances with him.
She puts on the record,
'Red Roses for a Blue Lady'
and throws him across the room.
Mind you,
she never laid a hand on him,
only the wall laid a hand on him.

The first three words of the first line seem neutrally descriptive
but 'bad', which pretends to belong to this factual register, slides
us into a new one. It is really part of the vocabulary through
which mother and son collude in her abuse of him, as the horror
of the fifth line shows.

Then comes the comment voice, in 'mind you': the poem is
pretending to sound like a gossipy neighbour talking about the sit-
uation in cliché ('laid a hand on him'). In the next line, the poem
wakes the cliché up, using the odd metaphor ('the wall laid a hand
on him') to make clear what is going on from the boy's perspective.
It is not his mother abusing him, but the wall.

The next movement begins with five lines in a new, nursery-
school register, developing the mother-child note we heard in 'bad'.

He gets red roses in different places,
the head, that time he was as sleepy as a river,
the back, that time he was a broken scarecrow,
the arm like a diamond had bitten it,
the leg, twisted like a licorice stick,
all the dances they did together,
Blue Lady and Tommy.

The chanting repetition and images are those you use playing
with an infant. ('Be sleepy as a river.' 'Be a broken scarecrow.')
Again, the poem gathers up what these lines tell us (how often
this has happened, how at risk he is, how many parts of his body
have been hurt) in a register of romanticising comment: 'all the
dances they did together, / Blue Lady and Tommy.' The title it
gives the mother, picking up from that of the record, reminds us
that the mother, as well as her child, must be miserable, and in
deep psychological trouble.

The dramatic climax comes in the longest movement, the third,
when an injury lands him in hospital. At 'you fell', the poem gives

us what the mother says directly to the child, apparently (we have lots of her language indirectly), though there are no quotation marks to say so. Perhaps we are in the child's remembering head at this point, for we now have five lines implicitly from his perspective ('nice lady', 'big hospital'), which make clear he knows he could be saved but doesn't want to be ('because he didn't want to be sent away').

Again the words that might express his own uncontaminated perspective take on the register of their relationship ('he could talk fine'). The lines in comment register ('He never told about the music') close the moment at which he could have been rescued, and terminate any possibility of change.

> You fell, she said, just remember you fell.
> I fell, is all he told the doctors
> in the big hospital. A nice lady came
> and asked him questions but because
> he didn't want to be sent away he said, I fell.
> He never said anything although he could talk fine.
> He never told about the music
> or how she'd sing and shout
> holding him up and throwing him.

The poem lets us rest a moment, then moves to a separated coda, which is the emotional climax of what this poem is doing to the reader. Not action now, but explanation.

> He pretends he is her ball.
> He tries to fold up and bounce
> but he squashes like fruit.
> For he loves Blue Lady and the spots
> of red red roses he gives her.

The first three lines of this are in the register of their joint 'play', and reveal the centre of all the poem's pretending. The child is pretending to himself. He 'is her ball'. They also show what it costs him ('he squashes'). The poem ends with an explanation which begins in comment reg-ister, 'for he loves', before returning to the register of their complicity. Echoing the nursery rhyme 'Ring a Ring of Roses' which ends in 'all fall down', and with 'spots' that evoke the rhyme's possible origins in the Plague, the poem re-sees the injuries she inflicts as the flowers in their song. He feels, and maybe she feels too, that the 'red, red roses' are a present. Not from her to him: from him (at great sacrifice) to her.

Sounds Like May Not Be What It Is

Tone is the total of all the poem's registers and sounds – heard, unheard, unnoticed, the lot. And of all the relationships between them.

All these sounds are com-posed, that is, put together, like the limbs of Orpheus or Echo. This composed tone contains the poem musically just as white spaces contain it visually.

In the end, the tone of a poem makes its truth. But the poem's truth is also com-position. Is the mad cow telling the truth? Whose truth? Is she mad? Or is asking that question not what this poem is "about"? Is it about, in fact, not asking that question?

In relation to facts, poets and poems have always lied. The first time the Muses put in a literary appearance, during the eighth century BC, they told the Greek poet Hesiod, 'We know how to say many false things as if they were true. But we know how, when we want, to say true things.' [27]

One way of thinking about a Muse is as a shorthand for what controls the poem. For whatever you are writing "about", for the words that occur and what they get up to, for metaphor which conjures thing that are not what it says they are. Lies, is one way of looking at it.

But there is something the poem must be true to or it will not work, and that is the poet's own imagination. In this sense, poetry lies to tell a truth.

'My God,' said the composer Charles Ives, 'what has sound got to do with music? The instrument! There is the perennial difficulty, there is music's limitation. What it sounds like may not be what it is.' [28]

In poetry, too, the tone is a confected sound. What it sounds *like* may not be what it is. It may be full of sly or contradictory voices, like the collusive registers of 'Red Roses'. But the whole thing must persuade the reader it has a true relation to something. A true relation to the making of a poem, of course, but also to something in the world, or at least someone's subjective experience of it.

The poem's honesty may have nothing to do with the claims and assertions it contains; with what it seems, on the surface, to be "about". From that point of view, the poem is probably a pack of lies. Accepting there is truth there all the same is part of recognising that this poem 'is good'.

Like harmony, tension and the viola, 'tone' is about relationship. On all levels, including that between poem and reader. In the end it is tone that determines how a poem affects the reader.

And this, finally, is what I shall look at tomorrow: a poem's relation with its reader.

The Dative Case: On Communication, Giving Poems to Other People and the Desire To Be Understood – Or Maybe Sometimes Not

The Space, the Silence, and the Beast

Yesterday, discussing tone, I talked of a poem's social being. But how can a poem be social when you turn away from people to write it? 'What kind of beast would turn its life into words?' asks a poem by Adrienne Rich.[1] A beast which works alone – as in Simon Armitage's poem 'The Patent *(i.m. Michael Donaghy)*':

> Last night in the shed he was working late,
> perfecting light,
>
> inventing the light bulb that lasts and lasts.
> He believes in lamps
>
> which as well as giving an instant shine
> will illuminate over and over again
>
> and, far from being dim, the prototypes
> are surprisingly bright
>
> and functional too, being fused
> for domestic use.[2]

Or as Charles Simic put it in his memoir:

> The poet sits before a blank piece of paper with a need to say many things in the small space of a poem. The world is huge, the poet is alone, and the poem is just a bit of language, a few scratchings of a pen surrounded by the silence of the night.[3]

How does something constructed by someone alone in a shed at night become so 'surprisingly bright' for other people? How does a poem make a relationship with unknown readers?

By perfecting the tone, and everything *tone* entails – tension, harmony, heard and unheard echoes. But tone comes basically, I believe, from generosity, the dative nature of a good poem. It is through tone that we trust a poem to give us something valuable. In inflected languages like Latin, the dative or "giving" case marks *to* and *for*. Directly or indirectly, poems are made for readers. The light bulbs which illuminate our lives are 'fused for domestic use'.

I began two days ago with a news editor who mistrusted poets because they never say what they mean, and have been suggesting that what you get from poems is what they do not say. (Not in, as it were, so many words.) Most good poems want to communicate something. But different poets communicate this differently. 'We have different ways of addressing the table,' says Durcan to Heaney in a poem we read yesterday. Both are masters of tone ('no mean strikers of the ball') but have different relations to the table and give differently to the person on its other side.

Modernism changed some of the goalposts in this giving. It highlit the difficulties of communication and expanded the distance between poet and readers. The poet critic C.K. Stead has argued that at the beginning of the 20th century the relationship between poet and reader became a tug-of-war.

> Where the audience stood too close, demanding flattery rather than truth, the poets donned the hieratic robes of the aesthete, pushing their readers away... Where the humanising influence of a public seemed remote and insubstantial, so that the poet's view of the world was in danger of becoming too special and literary, they...beckoned readers towards them.[4]

Today's audiences are more varied now than ever in the history of poetry, in any language. Most good poems want to give, to communicate, something complex, and not be understood all at once. But who to? How do those light bulbs illuminate readers with widely different experiences of reading?

I once showed a draft of a poem to a friend, a scholar used to elucidating old poems in unusual languages but not to reading modern poems.

'I had to look so many words up,' he complained. At least, I thought it was complaining. 'And even when I did, I couldn't always see what you were doing with them in the context.'

'Thanks,' I said. 'That's useful.'

'Why?'

'I want to be clear,' I said.

'You want to be clear?' He was completely astonished. 'Surely not.'

It shocked me that he should think not being clear was one of my aims. From where I stand, you work on a poem because you want to make it better, sharper, clearer. There will be much more to its meaning than you are aware of at the time. If you knew what you "meant" to say you would not need to write it. 'I couldn't look myself in the eye,' said Michael Donaghy once, 'unless I used verse as a means of discovery, rather than a method of persuading my audience of what I thought I already knew.'

You don't want to shut the reader out of your discoveries, though you hope they will find other ones in it for themselves. Keats said we all mistrust poems that have a palpable design upon us, but though we hate designs upon us we do enjoy design. We are designing animals. Where's the balance, then, between something which explores and discovers and something which is (that horrible word) accessible? Accessible to whom? And maybe it will change them, anyway. 'A way of speaking, if it is any good,' said W.S. Graham, 'as it persists creates its understanders. Its early idiosyncracies become solid currency. It is alive, changing and organic. And at last works.'[5]

His own poem 'The Beast in the Space'[6] is about what lies between poet and reader. The poem begins peremptorily, ordering the reader – some unknown you – to 'shut up' and not suppose there is anyone 'on the other side of the words'.

Shut up. Shut up. There's nobody here.
If you think you hear somebody knocking
On the other side of the words, pay
No attention. It will be only
The great creature that thumps its tail
On silence on the other side.
If you do not even hear that
I'll give the beast a quick skelp
And through Art you'll hear it yelp.

What is between the 'you' and the 'me' is a 'great creature', a beast which lives, and 'thumps its tail', on 'silence'. To make 'you' hear this thump, the first stanza ends on a thumping rhyme, through which it evokes 'Art'.

The second nine-line stanza orders the reader to call this beast over. The reader, in other words, must take an initiative in order to make the poem theirs.

> The beast that lives on silence takes
> Its bite out of either side.
> It pads and sniffs between us. Now
> It comes and laps my meaning up.
> Call it over. Call it across
> This curious necessary space.
> Get off, you terrible inhabiter
> of silence, I'll not have it. Get
> away to whoever it is will have you.

The 'beast' is a 'terrible inhabiter of silence'. It 'pads and sniffs', in 'this curious necessary space' between the 'I' and 'you'. The speaker pushes it away, like a bothersome dog, towards the reader.

In the third slightly longer stanza, the 'I' has got rid of the 'terrible beast'.

> He's gone and if he's gone to you
> That's fair enough. The heavy moth
> Bangs on the pane. The whole house
> is sleeping and I remember
> I am not here, only the space
> I sent the terrible beast across.
> Watch. He bites. Listen gently
> To any song he snorts or growls
> And give him food. He means neither
> Well or ill towards you. Above
> All, shut up. Give him your love.

Acting out one version of transactions between poet and reader, the speaker transfers responsibility for the beast that has lapped up his own 'meaning'. If it has gone 'to you / that's fair enough' – and the speaker feels free to reveal more of his own context. A 'sleeping' house and another life-form, a 'moth' (either inside, trying to get out, or outside trying to get in) which 'bangs on the pane' like that beast's tail thumping the 'silence'.

But then the speaker 'remembers' he is not really 'here', in this house of a poem, at all. There is 'only the space / I sent the beast across'. He reverts to imperatives. 'Watch', he tells the 'you'. That 'beast' I have sent you 'bites'.

Then, echoing the poem's first words, he tells the 'you' to 'shut up, listen gently' to the beast, to the 'song' of its animal noises, and finally (another thumping end-rhyme, like a closing couplet in a Shakespearian monologue) to 'give' it 'your love'.

A poem creates its tone, making a relationship with the people to whom it is given, across a 'necessary silence': some 'space' where meaning lurks like a restless animal, dangerous and demanding, taking 'bites' out of poet and reader alike.

'Here is a not very clean copy of "The Beast in the Space",' wrote Graham to a friend, reproducing exactly the situation his poem describes:

> I think you should have it because you liked the strangeness of it (although, I suppose, every poem should have a strangeness) and remember (although you mustn't let the possible meaning of the poem *for you* be curtailed) that the poem is about the difficulty of thorough communication. OK. OK.[7]

He did not want to influence what the poem might mean to someone else, but did want to explain what he himself had thought it was about – that communicating is so difficult. Which is obvious ('OK. OK').

Maybe all good poems stage, in concentrated form, the 'difficulty of thorough communication' between a 'you' and a 'me'. But they also offer ways of reflecting on this difficulty. In Armitage's image for Donaghy's poems, they 'illuminate over and over again'.

A poem lives in and lives off the space between poet and reader. This poem belongs to them both, but after the poet has 'sent' it 'off' it belongs more importantly to the reader. That is where it is going to live: the poet has done it and done with it. Graham also said a poem 'comes into new life' through each new reader. 'It is brought to life by the reader and takes part in the reader's change.'[8]

We might compare a book signing. When I sign a book I've written, I think of the years it took to write and what I learned from writing it. Now those poems are contained within a 'cover,' in a book someone else has paid for. The poems belong to this reader to do what they like with. But they want me to write in it. I write 'to', or 'for', and their name. Then I write my own. My signature says, 'I am in here somewhere. There is something of me which I am giving you. It is now yours.'

This operation is an image for the more important event which happens when a reader makes a poem theirs by understanding. By giving it, as Graham's poem finally comes out and says, 'love'. There has to be trust in this relationship, in which 'you' and 'I' stand on either side of a written poem. 'If you want to be spoken to,' he wrote to a friend, 'alright. Here I am speaking to you from the other side of language.'[9]

The reader has bought the book. The money symbolises that even more expensive investment of energy, of understanding. A poem costs you. Readers have to trust they will get something from it. The poem, or the book, was one particular set of things for me while I wrote it. Now, for the reader, it is something else. By meeting it with their own thought and feeling, readers make it theirs.

I Say I Say I Say: the Bond between Language and Communication

This space between poet and reader has silence in it too. I do not know you. You know me only through written signs. There may be more than one beast in here. This is the silence of many possible interpretations.

We might compare that silence to yesterday's silent letters, which cause spelling problems for people learning the language, and are generated in any alphabet by the space between sounds, which are words spoken, and the signs which are the same words written. The new forms of communication created by the move from speaking to writing, creates new silences too.

Every reader will receive the beast of meaning differently, give it different food, make a different animal of it. 'The poem is not a handing out of the same packet to everyone,' said W.S. Graham, 'as it is not a thrown-down heap of words for us to choose the bonniest'.[10] But if everyone gets different things from it, is the poem communicating at all? Armitage's image for what Donaghy's poems get up to is illumination, not communication. Maybe communicating is not the kind of thing a poem does? What is communicating, for a poem?

John Ashbery said that when he changed his style, after the Fifties, to his expert, avant garde, eel-like darting through the flotsam of the American street, he wanted 'to stretch the bond between language and communication but not to sever it'.[11] We know there is a bond. In real life, people use language for many things, to advertise, obfuscate, show off, lie, evade, warn, tease or hide, but most fundamentally to communicate.

Philip Larkin, most slippery of communicators, once said that a poem 'simply' transferred emotion from poet to reader. 'To me, poetry should begin with emotion in the poet and end with the same emotion in the reader. The poem is simply the instrument of transference.'

We shouldn't trust this of course. What Larkin says may not be what he means. Anyway, no poem does anything 'simply'. But as we saw yesterday, poets play tricks with truth to reach a new truth of their own. 'You've said a writer must write the truth,' an interviewer once asked Larkin. 'Presumably the truth of his experience?' 'I was probably lying,' Larkin said, but then played with 'Beauty is Truth, Truth Beauty' from Keats' 'Ode to a Grecian Urn' to embroider what he meant:

> Every poem starts out as either true or beautiful. You try to make the true ones seem beautiful and the beautiful ones true. When I say true, I mean something was grinding its knuckles in my neck and I thought: God, I've got to say this somehow, I have to find words and I'll make them as beautiful as possible.[12]

'I've got to say this somehow' reminds us of Graham's word describing the space between 'I' and 'you': 'necessary'. Larkin implies (not necessarily truthfully) that the beauty of a poem – call it the craft – and its truth (its emotion perhaps) are opposites. The challenge is to bring them together.

So if a poem does manage to bring beauty and truth together, does it communicate emotion? 'A poem is not only emotion,' Larkin said instantly in the same interview, pushing the case for craft and for thought:

> You've got the emotion side, let's call it the fork side, and you cross it with the knife side, the side that wants to sort it out, chop it up, arrange it and either say thank you for it or sod the universe for it.[13]

As W.S. Graham says, 'A poem is made of words, not the expanding heart, overflowing soul or sensitive observer.'

But whether the poem says thank you or sod the universe, Larkin does at least say that it is *saying*. What sort of saying happens in a poem?

Simon Armitage's sonnet 'I Say I Say I Say'[14] creates a rhetorical platform from which it addresses its readers. At first, in the octave, it expresses the way it is hiding emotion by hiding its rhymes, deep inside the line: 'go', 'know', 'show'; 'wrists' and 'fist'; 'laugh' and 'bath' backed up by 'dark' and 'hard'; 'drink', 'lint' and 'pink'; 'up' and 'luck'.

> Anyone here had a go at themselves
> for a laugh? Anyone opened their wrists
> with a blade in the bath? Those in the dark
> at the back, listen hard. Those at the front
> in the know, those of us who have, hands up,
> let's show that inch of lacerated skin
> between the forearm and the fist. Let's tell it
> like it is: strong drink, a crimson tidemark
> round the tub, a yard of lint, white towels
> washed a dozen times, still pink. Tough luck.

The sestet makes clear what the speaker is really 'saying', in this poem whose title repeats 'I Say' three times. The rhymes 'rush forward' (like 'those at the back' of the audience) into the open, the end position. 'Tough', from the last line of the octave, foreshadows 'cuffs', the last word of the first line of the sestet. 'Bangles', just before it, is partnered by another end word, 'brambles'. 'Woods', in stress position before the caesura, is matched by 'good', which is then partnered by another end word, 'blood'. Which ends what the poem calls a 'punchline', the violence of which image it picks up.

> A passion then for watches, bangles, cuffs.
> A likely story: you were lashed by brambles
> picking berries from the woods. Come clean, come good,
> repeat with me the punchline 'Just like blood'
> when those at the back rush forward to say
> how a little love goes a long long long way.

The last line would be a classic rhyming pentameter couplet, but the three times repeated 'long' lengthens it to six beats. With a spin (as in Durcan's poem yesterday) on the saying 'a little goes a long way' (and an echo from the chorus line of the Neil Sedaka song 'A Little Lovin'), the speaker comes out and tells it 'like it is'. Suicide is being contemplated, because 'a little love' has 'gone'. How long the long way feels comes over in the lengthening of the line, and the repetition. And perhaps by the unheard rhyme 'away', which we catch from way and 'say', which is also the verb in the title.

The mournful 'long long long' (like Tennyson's triple 'Break, Break, Break' in a poem written after his friend Arthur Hallam's death) reflects the apparently pompous triple repeat of the title. This whole poem is not the rhetoric it seemed at the start, but a bitter valediction.

Poems negotiate the uncertainties of communication between a you and a me very differently. Many opening lines in poems by Michael Donaghy highlight these uncertainties by pitching a self and an other, an unknown 'I' and an equally unknown 'you', into utterly unknowable relations. We cannot know who the poem supposes us to be, any more than we know who or what the speaker is.

Please hang up. I try again.
'My father's sudden death has shocked us all'
even me, and I've just made it up.'
                    ('The Excuse')

Can I come in? I saw you slip away.
Hors d'oeuvres depress you, don't they? They do me.
                    ('Black Ice and Rain')

I'd swear blind it's June 1962.
Oswald's back from Minsk. U2s glide over Cuba.
                    ('My Flu')

Don't be afraid old son, it's only me
though not as I've appeared before,
on the battlements of your signature
or margin of a book you can't throw out.
                    ('Haunts')

Donaghy pares the scenario of a poem to its emotional essentials, so we attend not to its literal truth but the feelings which it transfers (in Larkin's word) to us. Charles Olson also used that image of tranferring, describing a poem as a 'discharge of energy transferred from where the poet got it all the way to the reader'.[15]

We began two days ago with 'metaphor', whose Greek root means 'carrying across'. Now we end up with 'transference', whose Latin root means the same thing.

Maybe what a poem communicates is not fact or even feeling, but the energy of feeling. Maybe in every good poem, the underlying movement is towards finding a new route through that strange space, of infinite and dangerous uncertainties and meanings, which belongs to all communication between 'you' and 'me'. And when a poem 'says' successfully, it transfers an energy of feeling across this space.

Is that it? Not all readers will respond to this energy, but if the poem is good, many will. What they will make of it and take from it, however, will be different.[16]

At the Screen Door

Transferring is not the same as giving. The poem may *transfer* energy: poet and reader may both agree that it has energy. But a gift has emotional overtones too. Clouds of intention, conscious and unconscious, surround it. What do poets think they are giving? What a poet sees in the poem when giving it to a magazine to print, or speaking it to audiences, may not be at all what the audience or magazine-readers feel they have been given. 'I know what I have given you,' said the aphorist Antonio Porchia. 'I do not know what you have received.'

Yesterday, we talked of what the poem gives the reader in terms of sound. W.S. Graham describes a poem as 'the replying chord to the reader,' and 'the reader's involuntary reply'.[17] But what else, along with sounds, does the poem give?

Let's go back to the light-bulb-maker.

The uncertainty of communication was always a component in Michael Donaghy's poems but he also brought out our need to communicate. We we need to meet, in poems for example, and to find delight in meeting. His poem 'The Last Tea of Rikyu' suggests how much is at stake when we encounter each other in the 'tea hut' of a poem and take part in the ceremonies of giving and receiving, meaning and interpreting.

Early evening and a summer presence.
A moist wind moves on the roofs of Horyu-Ji,
Flicks iridescent beetle wings beneath wrought copper;
It is the daily rainstorm.

But we are in the tea hut in Rikyu's garden.
Rikyu, slandered without grace or respect,
Condemned by a dull and intolerant patron,
Is granted an hour of life.

The whirr of insects,
The master's hands, the lanterns,
And the damp hiss of the kettle
Show forth from the moment.

We take our places.
        'Do not be sad.
        We will meet every time there is tea.'
The unsteady cup warms my hands.

The others withdraw like shadows.
I remain to witness the gesture.
Rikyu unwraps bands of black silk
From the short sword.

His eyes are clear.
        'Have we not already died
        Who live beyond fear and desire?'
I weep for humility and gratitude

And do not see the shock, the body buckling.
This is how it always begins;
A jolt, the world whirls within us,
A raindrop hesitates, then hits the roof.[18]

At one level, like so many of Donaghy's poems, this poem
explores what it is to get the intricacies right in a poem. It moves
towards the moment of hara kiri through tiny details: beetle
wings, a kettle's 'hiss', the 'whirr' (presaging the 'whirl within' as
the blade hits the gut) 'of insects'.

Outside the poem, things are tough. Life is a 'daily rainstorm',
there is slander 'without grace or respect', condemnation from the
'dull and intolerant'. But we have poems. 'We meet every time
there is tea.' For both reader and poet, master and disciple, poems
can resemble the enclave of 'something understood' described in
George Herbert's poem 'Prayer'.

We 'take our places', poem and reader, meaning and interpreting, over the transfer whose image is the cup in 'my hands', received from 'the master's hands'. It 'warms' but is also 'unsteady', for this speaker insists on placing responsibility for action on the outside world: 'a summer presence, a moist wind, a patron'. The emotion builds through baldly named external objects: 'insects, lanterns; a jolt, the world; a raindrop'. Since the speaker experiences pain and uncertainty as coming from outside, it is the 'cup', not his 'hands', which is 'unsteady'.

The master's 'eyes', though, are 'clear'. The disciple 'weeps' and does not see the suicide; the poem sees it as a beginning ('this is how it always begins / a jolt') and finally moves on, in the last line, to a joke, a cliché which describes a snapping, someone unable to bear any more.

The subject of 'hits' is not a sword but a particle of the rainstorm of the first stanza. The only hesitation, and the only violence, is done by of 'a raindrop', which suggests a human counterpart, the tears of the disciple.

William Blake said poets were custodians of 'the holiness of minute particulars'. Through the minute particulars of the tea ceremony, and the ceremony by which the 'master' leaves life, this poem draws attention to the meticulous details by which it is made. This is what it gives the reader: the silent music of words which 'witness the gesture' and 'show forth from the moment'.

In one poem we looked at two days ago, Emily Dickinson's speaker says she dwells 'in possibilities'. Maybe this is what a poem is giving us: possibilities of finding meaning in it for ourselves. Everyone will find their own meanings, for instance, in Anne Carson's poem 'Screendoor' (*Autobiography of Red*, v).

In this poem, as in Graham's 'The Beast in the Space', something crosses from one person to another. A 'voice' floats across a 'shadowy kitchen' and affects somone in a way he will 'remember' for years to come.

His mother stood at the ironing board lighting a cigarette and
    regarding Geryon.

————

Outside the dark pink air
was already hot and alive with cries. *Time to go to school*, she said
    for the third time.

Her cool voice floated
over a pile of fresh tea towels and across the shadowy kitchen to
        where Geryon stood
at the screen door.
He would remember when he was past forty the dusty almost
        medieval smell
of the screen itself as it
pressed its grid onto his face. She was behind him now. *This would
        be hard*
for you if you were weak
but you're not weak, she said and neatened his little red wings and
        pushed him
out the door.[19]

What possible meanings offer themselves as I read this? First, I
am in a child's world. A 'mother' is at the ironing board: something
with 'iron' in it, something which flattens, but which she is not this
minute using. Her actions are ambiguous, 'lighting a cigarette',
'regarding Geryon'.

The child's name is strange and 'regarding' is not a child's word.
I feel I am both inside and outside his childhood perceptions.

Secondly, it is 'hot'. It could be evening with that 'dark pink
air', but 'already' suggests it is morning, a world waking up. The
'air' is sensuous, a presence in itself, 'alive'. How much of this is
the child's feeling at the time, how much objective description,
how much adult retrospect ('remember when he was past forty')?
I can't yet tell. But I suspect 'hot' says something about what is
being felt, as well as the outer environment.

'Time to go to school' and 'for the third time' tell me more.
This mother-child confrontation has been going on for some time.
In contrast to the air outside, her voice is 'cool'. 'Floated' sounds
effortless; the 'tea towels' show she has been using that 'ironing
board', working to keep things 'fresh'. As far as the child's per-
ceptions are concerned, any heat in the scene is in him, not her.
This country must have a lot of insects, mesh is needed to sepa-
rate inside from outside. But the 'screen door' his face pressed
against seems to stand for something he has to go through in some
sense I cannot know.

Between the two of them is that 'shadowy kitchen'. This moment
is traumatic ('remember…past forty'). What he will 'remember' is a
'dusty almost medieval smell'. 'Medieval', coming in an implicitly

traumatic setting with 'pressed', 'grid' and 'face' immediately after, makes me think of torture. Is he feeling tortured?

'She was behind him now' adds to my feeling that he feels she is torturing him, but is he right to feel that? Is she also 'behind him' in another sense, supporting him in what he must do? Why will he remember this moment all his life?

'This would be hard for you.' Aha – she is being cruel, but also (maybe only in her own view) sympathetic. She knows this is 'hard' for him but denies it. Why? To strengthen him to go 'out the door'? Or just make it easier for her? She gives him a self-image, 'not weak', to go to school with. She is looking after him, 'neatening' his psyche just as she ironed the tea towels. But then I find out, both why he's 'not weak', and why he does not want to go to school. All is explained by 'little red wings'.

This poem is from a book-length sequence, *Autobiography of Red*, which mirrors an ancient myth in a modern life.

The story is the Greek myth of Geryon, a red winged monster who loses his life in fighting the hero Herakles. Carson re-imagines Geryon as a modern North American boy who feels different from other people because he has red wings. He is bullied by his older brother, finds school difficult, is seduced and abandoned by an older boy, Herakles. At one level, the red wings are an image of the alienation Geryon feels because he is different. Eventually in the book, we feel one reason for that might be because he is gay.

But all children have moments of feeling different. Feeling different sometimes is part of learning how to be normally human.

Read on its own like this, without the rest of the book, the poem seems mysterious. Not because of difficult words, there is nothing unfamiliar except the child's name, but from the build-up of un-spoken emotions, leading to the oddity of 'red wings'. But when-ever I watch new readers coming to it fresh in a workshop, I admire afresh the way it gives the readers, even without knowing the myth, the background of the book, something they can trust and learn from.

What it gives, I think, is insight into that moment when a child is propelled 'out' into the world to deal with his own strangeness there alone. By its tone, which presents this child's particular strangeness matter of factly as normal, the poem offers new ways of thinking about what we all do. We all have to go 'out', and deal with the unique strangenesses we carry, through a door which separates us from the world but which is also a 'screen': something you can see and feel the world through. You can press your face against it, be hurt by it as by a grid. It might shelter you, too. 'Screen' can mean protect. But it is also something on which images get projected, like a mask or a persona, a version of self like the one Geryon will have to create for himself, to get through school.

Persona, the implied speaker from which the tone of a poem apparently proceeds, was a key concept for Ezra Pound. Browning's *Dramatis Personae* of 1855, poems written from the perspective of different dramatic characters, was a crucial influence on Pound's development as a poet. In 1909, Pound entitled his important third volume of poems *Personae*. The title gave him a schema with which to work, taking historical 'characters' as the speakers of lyrics like an opera aria. *Personae* said the 'I' in these poem was not the poet.

The original meaning of the Latin word *persona* (from *per*, 'through', and *sonare*, 'to sound') was 'mask'. It is a theatre image: *Personare* is 'to sound through'. On stage, words and voice 'sounded through' the mask's open mouth. And so *persona* also came to mean the 'stage figure' through whose voice and words you know the 'character'.

A poem, or book of poems, whose surfaces you have tried to polish till they hum, is a very public thing. It is words on stage. But even with all the worked intricacies, dramatic situations, shifting registers, third-person voices and multiple personae, the poem has still been made in that private garden shed or echo's cave of one poet's making self. As it comes out onto the public stage, it becomes part of the persona and the voice of that particular poet.

Poems, too, have to go out the screen door.

The Crossing Flow: Unnamed and Unnameable

But what about poems which seem not to want to communicate? Modernism questioned our relation to words. When John Ashbery said he 'wanted to stretch the bond between language and communication but not to sever it,' he was comparing himself with the Language (or L=A=N=G=U=A=G=E) poets who emerged in America in the late 1960s. For them, poems were constructions in language without reference to the outside world, and language itself was, as Ashbery puts it, 'more or less an independent entity, a free-standing object not concerned with communicating'. That position, he adds, 'is to the left of my own'.[20]

What are words doing, apart from merely being beautiful, in a poem that does not want to communicate?

Ashbery himself called the space where reader and poet meet 'a neutral ground, where the poet can begin operations',[21] and part of what his poems share, on this neutral ground, is the inner labyrinth of elusive feelings responding to the outer labyrinth of a material world whose meanings (both in itself and for us) we never entirely know. As in this passage from his poem 'The Wave':

> There's the moment years ago in the station in Venice,
> The dark rainy afternoon in fourth grade, and the shoes then,
> made of a dull crinkled brown leather that no longer exists,
> And nothing does, until you name it, remembering...

But some Modernist poems seem to shut a reader out completely, as if despairing that words ever name anything truthfully. The priest of that Modernist despair is Samuel Beckett. In his trilogy of novels, each new narrator is (or may be) revealed as the alias of the last. At the end, what is left is the voice of the Unnameable. Who or what is the Unnameable? Our 'blind need for words,' says one reader, 'plus the abiding sense that words name nothing, are only words'.[22]

Words cannot reproduce the world. It is falsifying to try and make out of them a poem that other people can understand because neither the world, nor our experience of it, is comprehensible. That, I think, is the idea. But I think something *is* communicated, even by poems that proceed from that premise. In this passage from J.H. Prynne's *The Oval Window*, words and their relationships seem to be counters whose shifts, fascinatedness, moments of exhilaration and surprise, mirror not the world, but the way we experience it.

I may be wrong but this poem belongs to me as a reader and what it seems to me to give is a sense that we cannot shape or control our experience of life any more than a reader can shape and control their reading of its words. That we live, as we read, in what it calls a 'crossing flow' of words, moments, perceptions, and that how we read is a model for how we experience living.

Standing by the window I heard it,
while waiting for the turn. In hot light
and chill air it was the crossing flow
of even life, hurt in the mouth but
exhausted with passion and joy. Free
to leave at either side, at the fold line
found in threats like herbage, the watch
is fearful and promised before. The years
jostle and burn up as a trust plasma.
Beyond help it is joy at death itself:
a toy hard to bear, laughing all night.[23]

I have no idea what 'trust plasma' is doing but I respond to the 'years' which 'jostle and burn up'. My understanding of the words is partial but I suspect that's the point: that our reading of the world is also partial.

The passage is part of a sequence which uses information technology and computer lore in a quest for a new response to the world, one which is not bossed around by traditional conventions of reading, electronic circuitry, or systems of commerce:

Pity me! These petals, crimson and pink,
are cheque stubs, spilling chalk in a mist
of soft azure.

What the words seem to communicate is a vision: that it is possible to find, in the rebarbative communication systems surrounding us as in our own exhausting emotions, corresponding moments of lyric.

Words are ambiguous. We all respond differently to the further ambiguities created when words get together. Everyone's ears are attuned to different things. Someone mentioned yesterday the role instinct plays, in responding to a poem. Instinct is what we start with and go on with, but instincts (as in a hunting dog) can be trained. We can all learn to read better, and trust a wider range of poems.

But your instinct is your own. It is you, not anyone else, making the relationship with this poem. Poetry today is so various because we, its readers, are various too. What kind of beast turns its life into words? Lots of different kinds. One overwhelming feature of poetry in Britain at the moment is its amazing variety. Which of course reflects the wildly varied reading experiences into which today's poems travel; and to which they want to give.

What's Love in All This Debris?

Marianne Moore's poem 'Poetry' opens by taking the side of a reader who apparently dislikes the light bulb making, the ceremonious detail, of poems. 'I, too, dislike it: there are things that are important beyond all this fiddle.' That word reminds us of Eliot's worries about writing *Little Gidding* during the blitz. Is poetry that important? If so, why?

In her second line, Moore's speaker begins to answer that question, switching to the impersonal one rather than I, as if impersonality will bring such convincing universality to the argument that readers, too, will change their mind.

> Reading it, however, with a perfect contempt for it, one discovers in it after all, a place for the genuine.[24]

So let's look, in our last ten minutes, at two poems which discover new ways of turning this space between poet and reader into a place for the genuine.

In her poem 'Yes Officer',[25] Carol Ann Duffy turns on its head the way the reader might not believe the literal truth of a poem. The poem's 'you' is a silent interrogator forcing a false confession out of the 'I'. In the end, the speaker's words become 'your' words and admit what the readers know (because they have shared the process) is forged and false.

> It was about the time of day you mention, yes.
> I remember noticing the quality of light
> beyond the bridge. I lit a cigarette.
>
> I saw some birds. I knew the words for them
> and their collective noun. A skein of geese. This cell
> is further away from anywhere I've ever been. Perhaps.
>
> I was in love. *For God's sake, don't.*
> Fear is the first taste of blood in a dry mouth.
> I have no alibi. Yes, I used to have a beard.
>
> No, no. I wouldn't use that phrase. The more you ask
> the less I have to say. There was a woman crying
> on the towpath, dressed in grey. *Please.* Sir.
>
> Without my own language, I am a blind man
> in the wrong house. Here come the fists, the boots.
> I curl in a corner, uttering empty vowels until

they have their truth. That is my full name.
With my good arm I sign a forgery. Yes, Officer,
I did and these, your words, admit it.

The violence, like the words voiced by the Officer, happens in silences between the words. Between 'anywhere I've ever been' and 'Perhaps'; between 'I have no alibi' and 'Yes, I used to have a beard'. They are part of the to-and-fro on a journey to a false confession.

The relation between poem and reader here is the opposite to that in Graham's 'Beast in the Space'. Instead of being bossy, and sending a terrible beast towards the reader, the speaker shrinks back 'in a corner, uttering empty vowels until / they have their truth'.

The silent and violent 'you' is unbearably intrusive. The speaker's actual memories ('I saw some birds'; 'I was in love'; 'There was a woman crying') are no help. 'Without' his 'own language' he is losing the power to say his own words. 'The more you ask / the less I have to say'. We know exactly what is going on but as in Sexton's 'Red Roses', yesterday, the poem does not say so in words. It reveals what is happening, challenging the truth of words which seem to belong to both 'you' and 'me'.

The title of Jo Shapcott's poem 'Phrase Book' [26] highlights a fragment of language. A 'phrase' is a few words that belong together. Not a grammatical sentence but not words on their own, either. Musically, a phrase is a short passage of notes which belong together but again, not a whole piece.

The poem brings out the estranging effects of language, in any relationship: in war, sex, or a foreign country. It mixes up three sorts of phrase: from euphemistic military jargon, from an old-fashioned handbook for a foreign language, and from a fraught romance whose lovers are increasingly a foreign country to, and maybe at war with, each other.

The first two verses begin with the speaker taking a 'stand' inside her identity, her 'skin', nationality, and 'front room', facing multiple scenarios: 'live' TV coverage of a war, people who speak a different language, and someone she does not 'understand'. For every possibility ('You are right') there is always the opposite alternative. 'You are wrong.'

I'm standing here inside my skin,
which will do for a Human Remains Pouch
for the moment. Look down there (up here).
Quickly. Slowly. This is my front room

where I'm lost in the action, live from a war,
on screen. I am Englishwoman, I don't understand you.
What's the matter? You are right. You are wrong.
Things are going well (badly). Am I disturbing you?

The next three verses make the three different languages clash.
The word that might describe the happiness of love-making, as it
was previously 'in this very room', is now an acronym for fighter
pilots. When the lover, the expected 'young gentleman', arrives in
the poem's central stanza, what will happen?

TV is showing bliss as taught to pilots:
Blend, Low silhouette, Irregular shape, Small,
Secluded. (Please write it down. Please speak slowly.)
Bliss is how it was in this very room

when I raised my body to his mouth,
when he even balanced me in the air,
or at least I thought so and yes the pilots say
yes they have caught it through the Side-Looking

Airborne Radar, and through the J-Stars.
I am expecting a gentleman (a young gentleman,
two gentlemen, some gentlemen). Please send him
(them) up at once. This is really beautiful.

But 'really beautiful' gives way to 'the Kill Box'. The scenarios
are getting muddled up as well as the different vocabularies. There
is more than one screen. Those 'pilots', seen in the 'war on screen'
in the second stanza, have now 'seen us…on their screens'.

The next two stanzas blur the speaker's 'front room' with the
'single room' where the pilots "take out" their targets. The speak-
er is surrounded by her baggage.

Yes they have seen us, the pilots in the Kill Box
on their screens, and played the routine for
getting us Stealthed, that is, Cleansed, to you and me,
Taken Out. They know how to move into a single room

like that, to send in with Pinpoint Accuracy, a hundred Harms.
I have two cases and a cardboard box. There is another
bag there. I cannot open my case – look out,
the lock is broken. Have I done enough?

The last two verses go back to that 'bliss' of the romance at its
high point, which has now turned destructive. It is the personal
arena, not the war, which lets euphemism give place to the lan-
guage of violence: 'one person pounding another into dust'. Faced
with that violence, the speaker ends in a volley of anxious ques-
tions.

Bliss, the pilots say, is for evasion
and escape. What's love in all this debris?
Just one person pounding another into dust,
into dust. I do not know the word for it yet.

Where is the British Consulate? Please explain.
What does it mean? What must I do? Where
can I find? What have I done? I have done
nothing. Let me pass please. I am an Englishwoman.

Through the different languages and scenarios, between the
screens of pilots 'getting us Stealthed' and a 'TV... showing bliss',
this is someone hanging desperately onto her identity. She may
move from 'standing here' in her 'own front room' to 'two cases
and a cardboard box', and a 'broken' lock, to asking to 'pass', but
she still knows who she is. 'I am an Englishwoman.'

The 'you' shifts confusingly through the different vocabularies.
It is the person the speaker does not 'understand', who is both
'right' and 'wrong', and to whom anxious orders are addressed.
'Please write it down...please send him (them) up.' Some 'you'
becomes amalgamated with me in 'us', as target of those 'pilots',
and then separated out again ('Cleansed, to you and me').

Love, the repricocity of 'you' and 'me', becomes 'one person
pounding another into dust'. That is why the speaker has to get
out – with five more questions and more imperatives to an un-
specified you. 'Let me pass please.'

Poems, says Charles Simic, 'are other people's snapshots in
which we recognise ourselves'. Modern poets assume, he says,
'that each self, even in its most private concerns, is representa-
tive'.

The self which Shapcott's poem reveals, in that curious space between the 'I' of a poem and the 'you' of a reader, represents the reader's self too: a self bombarded by relationship in three dimensions at once. The poem addresses 'a hundred Harms', the pressures of relationship on all of us, by revealing the fracturing that goes on between different kinds of 'phrase', and different ways of meeting each other, love and war, 'body to mouth', 'pounding to dust', 'evasion and escape'.

'Lyric poets perpetuate the oldest values on earth,' says Simic. 'They assert the individual's experience.' The technical, formal ways in which a poem stages its relationship with the reader – the ways in which it meets, gives to, plays with, evades, winks at, teases, entertains and becomes trusted by an audience – create a little lit stage, an image for all the ways we deal with ourselves and each other. The poem, says Simic, 'is a place where the "I" of the poet, by a kind of visionary alchemy, becomes a mirror for all of us'. [27]

'What's love in all this debris?' The aesthetic questions of a poem, and the uncertainties, ambiguities and formal delights we face both in writing and responding to it, are a microcosm for all human problems, relationships and pleasures. The poem gives. And the reader makes it theirs by loving it.

BIBLIOGRAPHY

John Ashbery, *Selected Prose* (Carcanet, 2004).
Mourid Barghouti, *I Saw Ramallah*, tr. Ahdaf Soueif (Bloomsbury, 2004).
Samuel Beckett, *Collected Poems in English and French* (Grove Press, 1977).
Samuel Beckett, *Texts for Nothing* (Calder and Boyars, 1999).
John Cage, *Silence* (Wesleyan University Press, 1961).
John Cage, *For the Birds: In Conversation with Daniel Charles* (Marion Boyars, Boston, 1981).
Janis Cull, *The Poem in Time: Reading George Herbert's Revision of 'The Church'* (University of Delaware Press, 1990).
Mahmoud Darwish, *A River Dies of Thirst*, tr. Catherine Cobham (Archipelago Books/Saqi Books, 2009)
T.S. Eliot, *Selected Essays* (Faber & Faber, 1951).
W.S. Graham, *The Nightfisherman: Selected Letters of W.S. Graham*, ed. Michael and Margaret Snow (Carcanet, 1999).
Seamus Heaney, *Preoccupations: Selected Prose 1968-1978* (Faber & Faber, 1980).
Seamus Heaney, *The Government of the Tongue: Selected Prose 1978-1987* (Faber & Faber, 1988).
Martin Heidegger, *Poetry, Language, Thought*, tr. Albert Hofstadter (1971; Harper Perennial, 2001).
Charles Ives, *Essays before a Sonata* (1st World Library, USA, 2004).
Richard Kostelanetz (ed.), *John Cage: Writer: Previously Uncollected Pieces* (Limelight, New York 1993).
James Knowlson, *Damned to Fame: The Life of Samuel Beckett* (Simon & Schuster, 1996).
Philip Larkin, *Further Requirements: Interviews, Broadcasts, Statements and Book Reviews*, ed. Anthony Thwaite (Faber & Faber, 2001).
John Livingston Lowes, *The Road to Xanadu: A Study in the Ways of the Imagination* (1927; Pan Books, 1978).
Louis MacNeice, *Varieties of Parable* (Cambridge University Press, 1965).
Dennis O'Driscoll, *Stepping Stones: Interviews with Seamus Heaney* (Faber & Faber, 2009).
Charles Olson, 'Projective Verse', *Poetry New York* (1950) No. 3.
Ruth Padel, *I'm a Man* (Faber & Faber, 2000).
Ruth Padel, *52 Ways of Looking at a Poem*, (Vintage, 2002).
Ruth Padel, *The Poem and the Journey* (Vintage, 2005).
Ezra Pound, 'A Retrospect,' in *Literary Essays of Ezra Pound*, ed. T.S. Eliot (Faber & Faber, 1954, 1960).
David Revill, *The Roaring Silence: John Cage: A Life* (Arcade, NY, 1992).

Adrienne Rich, *The Fact of A Doorframe: Selected Poems 1950-2001* (W.W. Norton, 2002).

Adrienne Rich, *What Is Found There: Notebooks on Poetry and Politics* (W.W. Norton, 2003).

I.A. Richards, *The Philosophy of Rhetoric* (Oxford University Press, NY, 1936, 1964).

Kaja Silverman, *The Acoustic Mirror: The Female Voice in Psychoanalysis and Cinema* (Indiana University Press, 1988)

Charles Simic, *A Fly in the Soup* (University of Michigan Press, 2002).

C.K. Stead, *The New Poetic: Yeats to Eliot* (1964; Continuum, 2005).

George Steiner, *On Difficulty and Other Essays* (Oxford University Press, NY, 1978).

Colm Tóibín (ed.) *The Kilfenora Teaboy: A Study of Paul Durcan* (New Island Books, Dublin 1996).

Calvin Tomkins, *The Bride and the Bachelors: Five Masters of the Avant-Garde* (Penguin/Viking, 1965).

Helen Vendler, *The Music of What Happens: Poems, Poets Critics* (Harvard University Press, 1988).

Helen Vendler, *Invisible Listeners: Lyric Intimacy in Herbert, Whitman and Ashbery* (Princeton University Press, 2005).

NOTES

FIRST LECTURE

1. Louis MacNeice, *Varieties of Parable* (Cambridge University Press, 1965), p. 3.

2. W.S. Graham, 'Notes on a Poetry of Release', appendix to *The Night-fisherman: Selected Letters of W.S. Graham*, ed. Michael and Margaret Snow, (Carcanet, 1999), p. 381.

3. Graham, 'Release', *Nightfisherman*, pp. 380-82.

4. *The Poems of Emily Dickinson: Reading Edition*, ed. Ralph W. Franklin (The Belknap Press of Harvard University Press, Cambridge, MA, copyright © 1951, 1955, 1979, 1983, 1998 by the President and Fellows of Harvard College), poem 986.

5. William Golding, *The Inheritors* (Faber & Faber, 1955).

6. *The Mill on the Floss* (1860), Book 2, Chapter 1.

7. Colm Tóibín, 'The Artist as Spring Lamb', in *The Kilfenora Teaboy: A Study of Paul Durcan*, ed. Colm Tóibín (New Island Books, Dublin, 1996), p. 19.

8. Adrienne Rich, *What Is Found There: Notebooks on Poetry and Politics* (W.W. Norton, 1993).

9. *The Poems of Emily Dickinson*, poem 657.

10. Aristotle, *Poetics* 1457B 7; I.A. Richards, *The Philosophy of Rhetoric* (Oxford University Press, New York, 1936, 1964), p. 96.

11. Seamus Heaney, *Preoccupations: Selected Prose 1968-1978* (Faber & Faber, 1980), p. 18.

12. Seamus Heaney, 'Making Strange' from *Station Island* (1984), from *Opened Ground: Poems 1966-1996* (Faber & Faber, 1998), pp. 221-22.

13. A shield has the same emblematic relation to Ares the war-god as a cup has to the Bacchus the wine-god. So one poet might call a shield 'the cup of Ares'. But another poet, an ancient Greek Durcan, for instance, might skip Ares entirely and simply refer to the shield as a 'wineless cup'. Aristotle, *Poetics* 1457B 16.

14. Martin Heidegger, *Poetry, Language, Thought*, tr. Albert Hofstadter (1971; Harper Perennial, 2001), p. 226.

15. *Selected Poems of Ezra Pound*, ed. T.S. Eliot, revised edition (Faber & Faber, 1948), p. 116.

16. Ezra Pound, 'Vorticism', *The Fortnightly Review*, 1 September 1914.

17. *Varieties of Parable*, pp. 105-06.

18. The term 'objective correlative' seems to have been invented by the American painter Washington Allston around 1840, in an 'Introductory Dis-

course' about the relation of 'the external world to the mind,' for his Lectures on Art. The mind, he said, needs 'some outward object' to be represented, which 'corresponds to a preexisting idea in its living power'. This produces a 'pleasurable emotion'. Eliot picked this up in his 1919 essay, 'Hamlet and his Problems'. He says there is something in Hamlet which Shakespeare cannot 'drag into the light, contemplate, or manipulate into art'; not, at least, as he did with Othello's jealousy. 'The only way of expressing emotion in the form of art is by finding an 'objective correlative'; in other words, a set of objects, a situation, a chain of events which shall be the formula for that particular emotion; such that when the external facts, which must terminate in a sensory experience, are given, the emotion is immediately evoked.' *Selected Essays* (Faber & Faber, 1951), pp. 144-45.

19. Ezra Pound, 'A Retrospect', Literary Essays of Ezra Pound, ed. T.S. Eliot (Faber & Faber, 1954), 3-14.

20. Louis MacNeice, *Varieties of Parable*, p. 105, quoting Graham Hough.

21. Ezra Pound, 'A Retrospect' (1918); Canto LXXXI.

22. See the debate I sketched out in *The Poem and the Journey*, pp. 13-14, 55, 244.

23. Dennis O'Driscoll, *Stepping Stones: Interviews with Seamus Heaney* (Faber & Faber, 2009), p. 449. See also Padel, *The Poem and the Journey*, pp. 244-45 on J.H. Prynne.

24. I wrote about this in a book which I took with me in bound proofs when I went to Burma for poetry workshops. Censorship there was an industry. Poems appeared in magazines with blacked-out words. No petals on boughs, because falling blossom might mean students killed in a demonstration. The poets, starved of books and new poetry, identified instantly with poets from elsewhere who had made great poems out of censorship. 'We have the mother of metaphor,' they said, quoting what I had read them: Borges's idea that 'censorship is the mother of metaphor'. See Padel, *52 Ways of Looking at a Poem* (Vintage, 2002), pp. 25-28, and 'The Wishing Stones: Poetry in Mandalay May 2002', *P.E.N. News* 2003.

25. See *52 Ways of Looking at a Poem*, pp. 28-32.

26. The Troubles was conflict within communities, different from occupation in Palestine provoking different poetic reactions. From that perspective, suggests Mourid Barghouti, 'Poetry that whispers and suggests can only be heard by free men', in *I Saw Ramallah*, tr. Ahdaf Soueif (Bloomsbury, 2004), p. 11.

27. David Harsent, *Legion* (Faber & Faber, 2005), p. 14.

28. Elizabeth Bishop, *Complete Poems* (Chatto & Windus, 1983), p. 131.

29. Elizabeth Bishop, *Complete Poems*, p. 79.

30. *The Poems of Emily Dickinson*, poem 303.

31. Don Paterson, *The Eyes* (Faber & Faber, 1999), p. 27.

32. Paul Durcan, *A Snail in My Prime: New and Selected Poems* (Harvill, 1993), pp. 131-38.

33. Samuel Beckett, *Collected Poems in English and French* (Grove Press, 1977), p. 73. I don't know why he loses the crucial word 'imagine' in his translation, since Beckett is so keen on 'imagination dead imagine', the title

of one of his short prose pieces, about 1965, in *The Complete Short Prose, 1929-1989*, ed. S.E. Gontarski (Grove Press, 1995).

34. James Knowlson, *Damned to Fame: The Life of Samuel Beckett* (Simon & Schuster, 1996), p. 352.

35. Samuel Beckett, *Texts for Nothing* (Calder and Boyars, 1999), p. 62.

36. ibid.

SECOND LECTURE

1. Louis Simpson, *Voices in the Distance: Selected Poems* (Bloodaxe Books, 2010), p. 68.

2. Seamus Heaney, *The Government of the Tongue* (Faber & Faber, 1988), pp. 107-08.

3. Heaney, ibid.

4. Seamus Heaney, *The Government of the Tongue*, p. 101; *Finders Keepers: Selected Prose 1971–2002* (Faber & Faber, 2002), p. 119.

5. Mahmoud Darwish, *A River Dies of Thirst*, tr. Catherine Cobham (Archipelago Books/Saqi Books, 2009), p. 139.

6. See Richard Kostelanetz, ed., *John Cage: Writer* (Limelight, NY, 1993), p. 43; *For the Birds: John Cage in Conversation with Daniel Charles* (Marion Boyars, Boston 1981) p. 43.

7. See John Cage, *Silence* (Wesleyan University Press 1961) p. 14; Richard Kostelanetz, ed., *Conversing with Cage* (Limelight, NY, 1988), pp. 44 & 189. He later added, 'In India they say music is continuous; it only stops when we turn away and stop paying attention', see David Revill, *The Roaring Silence* (Arcade, NY, 1992) p. 164.

8. John Cage, *Charles Eliot Norton Lectures* (Harvard University Press, 1990), p. 26; Kostelanetz, *Conversing with Cage*, p. 67; David Revill, *The Roaring Silence*, p. 164.

9. Richard Kostelanetz, *Conversing with Cage*, p. 42. See also p. 232.

10. David Revill, *The Roaring Silence*, p. 166; Calvin Tomkins, *The Bride and the Bachelors* (Penguin/Viking 1965), p. 119.

11. C.K. Williams, *Collected Poems* (Bloodaxe Books, 2006), pp. 197-98.

12. Paul Durcan, *A Snail in My Prime: New and Selected Poems* (Harvill, 1993), pp. 243-44.

13. Coleridge, *Biographia Literaria*, Ch xiii. He also says Fancy 'brings together images which have no connection natural or moral, but are yoked together by the poet by means of some accidental coincidence'. See Lowes, *The Road to Xanadu*, p. 320, who depicts sensations, images, phrases and words dropping into Coleridge's unconscious as into a well, collided with other images bobbing round in there, stuck together in new combinations, bubbled to the surface as a 'flash of association' and came up in poems as words.

14. Lowes associates Poincaré's phrase 'hooked atoms' with Coleridge's phrase, 'the hooks and eyes of memory', *The Road to Xanadu*, pp. 312-24.

15. George Steiner, *On Difficulty and Other Essays* (Oxford University Press, NY, 1978), p. 21.

16. Charles Olson, 'Projective Verse', *Poetry New York* (1950) No. 3.

17. Plato *Republic* 431E-432A, *Phaedo* 86B.

18. *The Merchant of Venice*, V. 1. 70-88.

19. B not pronounced after M in words like climb. C before L in words like muscle. D in words like handkerchief or Wednesday. G before N as in champagne, sign. GH, not pronounced before T and at the end of words like thought, through. H after W (what), and at beginnings (hour, r honest). K when followed by N at a beginning (knife). L before D, F, M, K (calm, half, talk, would). N after M at the end (autumn, hymn). P at the beginning of Greek-derived words starting 'psych' or 'pneu'. S before L in words like island. T after an S or F (castle, listen). W at beginnings, after an R (write) or before H (who).

20. *The Poems of Emily Dickinson*, poem 632.

21. Helen Vendler, *Invisible Listeners: Lyric Intimacy in Herbert, Whitman and Ashbery* (Princeton University Press 2005) p. 22; Janis Cull, *The Poem in Time: Reading George Herbert's Revision of 'The Church'* (University of Delaware Press, 1990) p. 134.

22. *Romeo and Juliet*, II. 2. 161-63.

23. Wordsworth, *Prelude*, V, l. 395-403; Seamus Heaney, *The Government of the Tongue*, pp. 153-59.

24. See Kaja Silverman, *The Acoustic Mirror: The Female Voice in Psychoanalysis and Cinema* (Indiana University Press, 1988); Ruth Padel, *I'm a Man* (Faber & Faber, 2000), pp. 292-93.

25. James Wright, *Above the River: The Complete Poems* (Bloodaxe Books, 1992), p. 133.

26. W.S. Graham, Letter to Ruth Hilton, 21 March 1967, *Nightfisherman*, p. 210.

27. Selima Hill, *Gloria: Selected Poems* (Bloodaxe Books, 2008), p. 105.

28. Jo Shapcott, *Her Book: Poems 1988-1998* (Faber & Faber, 2000), p. 69.

29. Anne Sexton, *The Complete Poems* (Houghton Mifflin, 1981), pp. 492-93.

30. Hesiod, *Theogony*, 27-28.

31. Charles Ives, *Essays before a Sonata* (1st World Library, USA, 2004), pp. 106-07.

THIRD LECTURE

1. In 'Twenty-One Love Poems' from *The Dream of a Common Language* (1978), in Adrienne Rich, *The Fact of a Doorframe: Selected Poems 1950-2001* (W.W. Norton, 2002), p. 146.

2. Simon Armitage, *Tyrannosaurus Rex versus The Corduroy Kid* (Faber & Faber, 2006), pp. 48-49.

3. Charles Simic, *A Fly in the Soup* (University of Michigan Press, 2002), p. 160.

4. C.K. Stead, *The New Poetic: Yeats to Eliot* (1964; Continuum, 2005), p. 3.

5. W.S. Graham, Letter to Ruth Hilton, 21 March 1967, *Nightfisherman*, p. 210.

6. W.S. Graham, *Collected Poems 1942-1977* (Faber & Faber, 1979), p. 147).

7. W.S. Graham, Letter to Ronnie Duncan, 22 October 1966, *Nightfisherman*, p. 200.

8. W.S. Graham, *Nightfisherman*, Appendix: 'Notes on a Poetry of Release', p. 382.

9. W.S. Graham, Letter to Robert Brennan, 24 January 1967, *Nightfisherman*, p. 207.

10. W.S. Graham, *Nightfisherman*, 'Release', p. 381.

11. John Ashbery, Robert Frost Medal Address in his *Selected Prose* (Carcanet, 2004) p. 251. See also Helen Vendler, *The Music of What Happens: Poems, Poets Critics* (Harvard University Press, 1988), p. 235.

12. Philip Larkin, Interview with John Haffenden, in *Further Requirements: Interviews, Broadcasts, Statements and Book Reviews*, ed. Anthony Thwaite (Faber & Faber, 2001), p. 49.

13. Philip Larkin, *Further Requirements*, p. 53.

14. Simon Armitage, *Dead Sea Poems* (Faber & Faber, 1995), p. 9.

15. Charles Olson, 'Projective Verse', *Poetry New York* (1950) No. 3.

16. Compare W.S. Graham on a poet whose work he says he does not respond to, but this is 'only me and only her'. 'About Stevie Smith I really don't know. Some poems say something, Others don't. It isn't the kind of poetry which really interests me, Too aphoristic. It makes no place or time or other world for me. But that's only me and only her.' Letter to Ruth Hilton, 7 January 1967, *Nightfisherman*, p.207.

17. W.S. Graham, 'Release', *Nightfisherman*, pp. 380-82.

18. Michael Donaghy, *Shibboleth* (Oxford University Press, 1988), p. 45.

19. Anne Carson, *Autobiography of Red* (Jonathan Cape, 1999), p. 36.

20. See above, note 11.

21. Talking of Marianne Moore, Ashbery said her subject was 'any in which she is interested and in which we might conceivably be interested. No more is necessary to establish a neutral ground where reader and writer may meet and the latter begin operations.' Ashbery p. 84.

22. Benjamin Kunkel, 'Sam I Am: Beckett's private purgatories', *The New Yorker*, 7 August 2006, pp. 84-90), p. 89.

23. J.H. Prynne, *The Oval Window* (1983), from *Poems*, second edition (Bloodaxe Books/Fremantle Arts Centre Press, 2005), p. 339.

24. *The Poems of Marianne Moore*, ed. Grace Shulman (Faber & Faber, 2003), p. 135.

25. Carol Ann Duffy, *Selling Manhattan* (Anvil Press Poetry, 1987), p. 37.

26. Jo Shapcott, *Her Book: Poems 1988-1998* (Faber & Faber, 2000), pp. 65-66.

27. Charles Simic, *A Fly in the Soup* (University of Michigan Press, 2002), p. 162.

BOOKS BY RUTH PADEL

POETRY
Alibi
Summer Snow
Angel
Fusewire
Rembrandt Would Have Loved You
Voodoo Shop
The Soho Leopard
Darwin: A Life in Poems
The Mara Crossing

ABOUT POETRY
52 Ways of Looking at a Poem
Alfred Lord Tennyson: Poems with Introduction and Notes
The Poem and the Journey
Sir Walter Ralegh
Silent Letters of the Alphabet

NON-FICTION
In and Out of the Mind: Greek Images of the Tragic Self
Whom Gods Destroy: Elements of Greek and Tragic Madness
I'm a Man: Sex, Gods and Rock 'n' Roll
Tigers in Red Weather

FICTION
Where the Serpent Lives